Smith, Marie.
N is for our nation's capital

2/06

N is for our Nation's Capital

A Washington, DC Alphabet

Written by Marie and Roland Smith and Illustrated by Barbara Leonard Gibson

Sleeping Bear Press

310 North Main Street, Suite 300
Chelsea, MI 48118
www.sleepingbearpress.com

© 2005 Thomson Gale, a part of the Thomson Corporation.

Thomson, Star Logo and Sleeping Bear Press are trademarks
and Gale is a registered trademark used herein under license.

Printed and bound in Canada.

10 9 8 7 6 5 4 3 2 1

Library of Congress Cataloging-in-Publication Data

Smith, Marie.
N is for our nation's capital : a Washington, DC alphabet / written by Marie and
Roland Smith ; illustrated by Barbara Gibson.
p. cm.
Summary: "An A-Z pictorial for children all about our nation's capital including
famous people, geography, history, and symbols. Topics are introduced with
poems accompanied by expository text to provide detailed information"—
Provided by publisher.
ISBN 1-58536-148-8
1. Washington (D.C.)—Juvenile literature. 2. English language—Alphabet—
Juvenile literature. I. Smith, Roland, 1951- II. Gibson, Barbara. III. Title.
F194.3.S555 2005
975.3—dc22   2004027814

*Dedicated to our family of veterans who served our country especially
Smitty, Hap, Mike, Granddad, Dad, Steve, Bob, Gary, and Shawn.*

MARIE & ROLAND

For my sister, Karen.

BARBARA

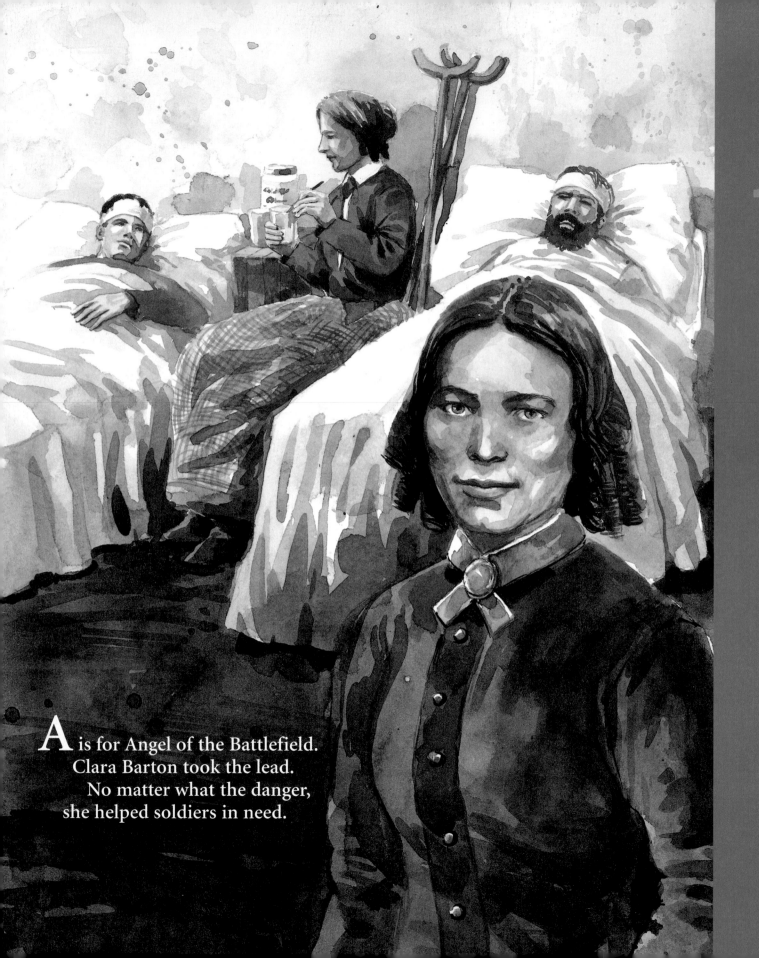

A is for Angel of the Battlefield.
Clara Barton took the lead.
No matter what the danger,
she helped soldiers in need.

Clara Barton was a clerk in the U.S. Patent Office in our nation's capital when the Civil War started. She began taking care of the soldiers and was given permission to travel where she was needed most—the battlefields. One night she arrived at a field hospital bringing a wagonload of supplies after a heavy battle. The surgeon on duty wrote later, "I thought that night if heaven ever sent out an angel, she must be one—her assistance was so timely." Soon after, she became known as the "Angel of the Battlefield."

Clara Barton helped start the American Red Cross. The home of the Red Cross is just a short distance from the White House and fills an entire block called Red Cross Square. It also has a monument for all women who cared for the sick and wounded during the Civil War and World War I.

A is also for Archives. The Declaration of Independence, the Constitution, and the Bill of Rights are just part of the treasures stored in our national Archives.

B is for the Blair House.
Here the president's guest,
while visiting our nation's capital,
has a place to rest.

Blair House was purchased for use as the official presidential guesthouse in 1942 after Eleanor Roosevelt found Winston Churchill in his nightshirt wandering the White House. He was hoping to meet President Roosevelt for breakfast!

Blair House was built in 1824 for Dr. Joseph Lovell, the first Surgeon General of the United States. The Blair family later purchased the house and held meetings here for many well-known Americans like John Calhoun, Henry Clay, Daniel Webster, and Jefferson Davis. Lincoln often visited here during his neighborhood walks. Blair House was where Robert E. Lee was offered, but refused, the command of the Union troops. Lee later became commander of the Confederate States Army.

Harry Truman, our 39th president, lived at Blair House while the White House was being remodeled. During his stay at Blair House an assassination attempt was made on his life. One officer was killed and two others wounded defending the president. Truman dedicated a plaque in front of Blair House to Leslie Coffelt, the officer who died while protecting him.

The president-elect stays at Blair House the night before his inauguration.

In 1912 First Lady Helen Taft and Viscountess Chinda, wife of the Japanese Ambassador, planted the first two cherry trees on the northern bank of the Tidal Basin. The cherry trees are still standing and are two of over 3,000 trees the people of Japan sent as a gift to the United States. In Japan the flowering cherry tree is called "*Sakura*" and is their national flower. The blooming of the cherry trees around the tidal basin and the Jefferson Memorial brings hundreds of thousands of visitors each year to our nation's capital.

The Tidal Basin is a pool originally dug by the Army Corps of Engineers during the 1880s to help with the yearly flooding of the Potomac River. The dredging of the river channel created new land that became the West and East Potomac Parks. Hains Point, the southernmost tip of East Potomac Park, was named after Major General Peter Hains, the engineer who directed the work.

C is for capital and capitol. Notice the difference in spelling? Washington, D.C. is our nation's capital city. The building where the Senate and House meet is our nation's Capitol Building.

C is for Cherry blossoms—
such a lovely view.
To the people of Japan,
we give our thanks to you.

D is for a Dream
of Martin Luther King.
He shared with everyone
"Let freedom ring."

Dr. Martin Luther King Jr. became known for his eloquent speeches and peaceful protests supporting civil rights in America. His most remembered speech called "*I have a dream*" was given on the steps of the Lincoln Memorial. He won the Nobel Peace Prize in 1964. The Martin Luther King Jr. Memorial Library located in our nation's capital has a museum with information about his life. Dr. Martin Luther King Jr. Day is an official holiday celebrated on the third Monday in January.

The Lincoln Memorial is in memory of Abraham Lincoln, our 16th president. Lincoln was called the "Great Emancipator" after he freed the slaves during the Civil War. His speeches are carved on the walls of his memorial. One, called the Gettysburg Address, starts out: "Four score and seven years ago our fathers brought forth on this continent, a new nation, conceived in Liberty, and dedicated to the proposition that all men are created equal..."

Another famous event on the steps of the Lincoln Memorial was the day Marian Anderson sang after she was denied the right to perform at Constitution Hall because she was African American.

Since 1878 an Easter Egg Roll has been on the south lawn of the White House. Before that it was on the lawn of the Capitol Building. All the children running around made the members of Congress unhappy about the expense and upkeep of the grass. Congress passed a law forbidding our nation's Capitol grounds to be used as a playground, disappointing a lot of children. President Hayes and his wife Lucy heard about the new law and unhappy children. They officially opened the White House grounds for egg rolling. Every president since has continued the tradition using the south lawn. A few times the event has been canceled during war and bad weather.

E is also for Ellipse, the White House south lawn, named for its shape. The space is also used for other outside activities, including ball games.

E is for the Easter Egg Roll
        behind the south lawn gate—
a White House tradition since
            President Hayes in 1878.

The statue of Freedom on the very top of our nation's Capitol Building stands on a globe of the world with our national motto, *E Pluribus Unum*. She is almost 20 feet tall and weighs over 7 tons. *E Pluribus Unum* is a Latin phrase meaning "Out of many, one." It refers to the 13 original colonies that became the United States. The statue of Freedom was placed on top of our nation's Capitol Building during the Civil War—a difficult time to finish any construction project. President Lincoln insisted it be finished—he said, "...it is a sign that the Union shall go on."

Our nation's Capitol Building is home to the Senate in the north wing and the House of Representatives in the south wing. Here they try to make laws that are good for everyone. Each state votes for representatives to send to Washington. The number of senators is limited to two per state, but the number of congressmen or congresswomen depends on the state's population.

F is also for flag. The flag for our nation's capital is a version of George Washington's family coat of arms.

F **f**

F is for Freedom.
During snow, rain, or sun
she guards the words we cherish
E Pluribus Unum—Out of many, one.

E. PLURIBUS UNUM

Gg

George Washington, our first president, is called the "Father of our country." He was the Commander of the Continental Army during the Revolutionary War and was unanimously elected president in 1789 and 1792. After choosing the exact spot for our nation's capital in the middle of swamp and farmland, he hired French engineer Pierre-Charles L'Enfant to draw a design for the new capital city. L'Enfant had served with Washington during the Revolutionary War. He wanted to create a capital, in his words, that was "magnificent enough to grace a great nation." One of the things these two men did together was choose the site for the new residence of the president. President Washington never lived in the house that became known as the White House and L'Enfant did not participate in the construction of his plans for the great city he envisioned.

The Washington Monument is an obelisk tower built to honor our first president. An obelisk is a tall four-sided pillar, usually with a pyramid-shaped top. The Washington Monument is 555 feet and 5⅛ inches high. It is the tallest structure in our nation's capital and was first opened to the public on October 9, 1888.

George Washington, our first president, starts with the letter G.
He planned our nation's capital and all that it would be.

H is for House—
the most famous in our nation.
1600 Pennsylvania Avenue,
everyone knows this location.

The White House has become a symbol of the presidency, the United States Government, and the American People—many presidents have called it "the People's House." The title White House did not become official until 1901. Before that, the house at 1600 Pennsylvania Avenue was called the President's House, Executive Mansion, or President's Palace. Our second president, John Adams, was the first to live in the White House.

The White House is the oldest public building in our nation's capital and was the largest house in the U.S. until after the Civil War. It is 55,000 square feet and has 132 rooms—35 of them are bathrooms—on 18 acres of land. It is not only where the president lives but also where he works. The president's office is called the oval office and is in the West Wing of the White House. The East Wing has the office of the First Lady. Parts of the White House are open to the public but not the top floor which contains the private quarters of the First Family.

An island in the Potomac River was considered a perfect place to honor our 26th president, Theodore Roosevelt. A 17-foot high statue of Theodore Roosevelt is standing near the center of the island. Parts of his speeches are carved in granite behind him. One of these is: "The Nation behaves well if it treats the natural resources as assets which it must turn over to the next generation increased and not impaired in value." He established the U.S. Forest Service and set aside over 230 million acres of public lands as national parks, forests, monuments, and wildlife refuges —the first president to do so. Once he refused to shoot a captured black bear. Soon after, stuffed bears called "Teddy's Bear" were being sold as popular toys. The island is considered part of our nation's capital but its entrance is on the Virginia side of the Potomac River.

President Theodore Roosevelt was the first American to win the Nobel Peace Prize after he negotiated an end to the Russo-Japanese War and was also the first president to use the phrase "White House" as an official title.

An Island in the Potomac River
has a statue 17 feet high,
named after Theodore Roosevelt.
Island starts with the letter **I**.

I **i**

J j

J is for Jazz.
We give recognition
to a man they called "the Duke,"
a D.C.-born musician.

Edward Kennedy Ellington, "the Duke," was born on April 29, 1899 in our nation's capital. When he was young he was more interested in baseball than piano but then he heard Harvey Brooks, a great pianist, and was inspired to learn how to play the piano. Duke Ellington started a group called the Duke's Serenaders that performed throughout D.C. He moved to New York and renamed his band the Washingtonians and traveled all over the world, giving over 20,000 performances. He once said, "If jazz means anything, it is freedom of expression." He was awarded the United States' highest civil honor, the Presidential Medal of Freedom, and the French government honored him with their highest award, the Legion of Honor.

Another famous D.C. musician was John Philip Sousa, born on November 6, 1854. His father, Antonio, was a musician in the Marine Band. When John was 13 he became an apprentice musician for the Marine Band and at age 26 became the bandleader. He wrote "The Stars and Stripes Forever," which was named as our national march in 1987. The Marine Band is America's oldest professional musical organization.

Kahlil Gibran, poet, philosopher, and artist was born in Lebanon in 1883, and later immigrated to the United States. His book *The Prophet*, published in 1923, has been translated into more than 20 languages. Over 8 million copies have been sold in the United States alone. Congress gave two acres of federal land located in our nation's capital for the Kahlil Gibran Memorial Garden in 1984 along Embassy Row. The garden has fountains, stone benches with Islamic script, and three cedar trees from Lebanon, their national symbol. Our 40th president, George H. Bush, gave the dedication speech when it was completed.

There are more than 170 foreign embassies in our nation's capital. Many of these are located on Massachusetts Avenue just north of the White House in an area known as Embassy Row. An embassy is the ambassador's official home. An ambassador is a representative from one country to another.

The vice president's house is also located on Embassy Row at the Naval Observatory.

K is for Kahlil Gibran,
a poet the world came to know.
A memorial garden for him
is located on Embassy Row.

L is for Library of Congress.
Here find all the books
published in the United States
filling each and every nook.

The Library of Congress is the largest library in the world and is located behind our nation's Capitol Building. The library was first started in 1800 to help members of Congress with research. President Thomas Jefferson sold his personal library to Congress as a replacement for the small collection of books that was destroyed during the War of 1812. Eventually three buildings were built for the library, each named after a president—the Thomas Jefferson, the John Adams, and the James Madison Building. Today the Library of Congress has nearly 128 million items on approximately 530 miles of shelves including recordings, photographs, maps, manuscripts, printed material, and of course books—over 200,000 of them are for children. The public cannot check out books but if you are over 18 you can use the books while in the library.

In our nation's capital, a small library can be found in the home and national historic site of Frederick Douglass, who lived from 1818 to 1895. He was an escaped slave, abolitionist, editor, orator, and public servant. His papers are on display in the Library of Congress.

Ll

M is for Mrs. Madison.
She said it was only right
George Washington's portrait
be safe before her flight.

During the War of 1812 the British attacked and set fire to our nation's capital. Before fleeing from the White House to safety, Dolley Madison, wife of James Madison our fourth president, saved many valuables. One of the most cherished items she saved was George Washington's portrait. She refused to leave until the portrait was taken down and sent to safety. The painting now hangs in the East Room of the White House.

Dolley Madison was known as a gracious hostess. She was the first wife of a president to be called "first lady" which later became the official title for the president's wife. She also was given her own seat in the House of Representatives, an honor never before given to any other American woman.

M is also for Mayor Walter Edward Washington. He was appointed mayor-commissioner of our nation's capital three times before he was elected mayor in 1975. He was Washington, D.C.'s first elected mayor in over a century and was the first African-American mayor of a major city in the United States.

N is for National Mall.
This is a place to play
or give a speech about anything
on any given day.

Pierre L'Enfant wanted open spaces and parklands for our nation's capital. Part of his plan is now known as the National Mall. It is a beautiful area with many trees, flowers, and ponds. Some of our presidents' memorials are here including the Washington Monument, the Lincoln Memorial, the Thomas Jefferson Memorial, and the Franklin D. Roosevelt Memorial. It has become a stage for national expressions of remembrance, observance, and protest. Something fun can be found on the Mall too. The Smithsonian Kite Festival is held on the Mall each year with kite fliers from around the world. Aviation pioneer Paul E. Garber started it.

N is for nation's capital. Washington is the capital city of the United States. It is not part of any state, but within a district called the District of Columbia, named after Christopher Columbus. The federal government manages it. George Washington originally called our nation's capital the Federal City, but people wanted to honor our first president and soon it was called Washington, the District of Columbia. Now we often refer to it as D.C., the Capital, or the District or sometimes just Washington—it has a lot of names!

On September 25, 1981, Sandra Day O'Connor became the first woman ever appointed to the Supreme Court. She grew up on a ranch started by her grandfather called the Lazy B in southeastern Arizona. It had 198,000 acres of land with more than 2,000 cattle. The house didn't have running water or electricity until Sandra Day was seven. Justice Day graduated from high school at 16. She went to Stanford University, first getting a degree in economics before studying law. She is the mother of three sons.

The Supreme Court is located behind the nation's Capitol Building. The Supreme Court is the highest court in the United States. It is made up of nine justices. To become a justice, a person must be nominated by the president and confirmed by a majority of the Senate. Once a justice is confirmed to the Supreme Court, the appointment is for life or until he or she resigns.

Our 27th president, William Taft, was appointed chief justice of the United States Supreme Court in 1921. He is our only president to serve on the court.

O is for O'Connor.
A member of the Supremes.
The first woman appointed
to our highest judicial team.

EQUAL JUSTICE UNDER LAW

P p

Powhatan was an Indian chief who lived in the early 1600s. Powhatan ruled about 30 native tribes known as the Powhatan Confederacy. They lived along rivers in and around the area that later became Washington, D.C. The rivers provided both food and transportation. Powhatan's daughter was Pocahontas and is remembered for her kindness and generosity to the first settlers that came here from England.

P is also for the Potomac River—the word "Potomac" comes from the Indian word meaning "where the goods are brought in," and is also the name of the rotunda, a major feature in the American Indian Museum, the Smithsonian Institute's newest building located on the National Mall. The rotunda is 120 feet high and 100 feet in diameter. It symbolizes the traditional gathering place of native people.

P is for Powhatan people.
They were here long before
anyone thought of our nation's capital
along the Potomac Shore.

President John Adams—
Which one? There were two.
First the father; then the son.
Thank goodness for the letter Q!

John Adams was the second president of the United States. His son, John Quincy Adams, was the sixth president. The Adams were the first father and son to be president. Our 41st president, George H. Bush, and our 43rd president, George W. Bush, were the second father and son to be president.

John Adams was our first vice president before he became president. In the state dining room of the White House inscribed on the mantel is a prayer he penned in a letter to his wife, Abigail—"I pray Heaven to bestow the best of blessings on this house and all that shall hereafter inhabit it. May none but honest and wise men ever rule under this roof." He died on July 4, 1826, the same day his friend and political rival President Thomas Jefferson died, 50 years after they both signed the Declaration of Independence.

John Quincy Adams became a congressman after being president. He was given the nickname "Old Man Eloquent" because of his powerful speeches on his opposition to slavery and his strong defense of freedom of speech.

Qq

R is for a flower.
In 1925 a commission chose
this fragrant symbol of D.C.,
the American Beauty Rose.

R r

The American Beauty Rose is a pink rose known for its fragrant smell. It is a favorite in the gardens of our nation's capital.

R is also for river. The Anacostia River flows through our nation's capital. Its name comes from the Indian word "*anaquash*," which means "village trading center." It was a river Native Americans used to catch shad, perch, herring, and other fish that were a staple of their diet. Sometimes people call it "D.C.'s forgotten river" because of all the pollution in recent years. But lately leaders in Washington, D.C. and Maryland, where the river starts, have been working together to reduce the river's pollution levels.

Francis Scott Key was a well-established lawyer in Georgetown, a suburb of our nation's capital. He appeared many times before the Supreme Court and had been appointed the United States District Attorney. During the War of 1812 he was asked to negotiate the release of Dr. William Beanes, who had become a prisoner of the British. The British agreed to release Beanes but not until after the bombardment of Fort McHenry.

After 25 hours of continuous bombing without capturing Fort McHenry, the British decided to leave. When the sun came out Key looked toward the fort to see if the American flag was still there. He was so grateful and moved when he saw the 30- by 42-foot flag still flying, he wrote down the words to a poem. The poem later became our national anthem. In 1931, our 31st president, Herbert Hoover, signed into law a bill that designated "The Star-Spangled Banner" as the U.S. national anthem.

The flag that inspired Francis Scott Key to write "The Star-Spangled Banner" is on display at the Smithsonian National Museum of American History.

S is for Star-Spangled Banner—
it inspired Francis Scott Key
to write the words we sing and cherish,
"O say, can you see,…"

The tradition of a national Christmas tree started in 1913. The first lighting had more than 20,000 people crowded into the East Plaza of our nation's Capitol Building to celebrate with the Marine Band, 1,000 singers and a live nativity scene. Our 30th president, Calvin Coolidge, was the first president to light the tree. Today the event is called the Pageant of Peace to symbolize our nation's desire to maintain peace around the world through the spirit and meaning of Christmas and is held on the Ellipse at the White House.

T is also for a tree called the Scarlet Oak, another symbol of our nation's capital. Its beautiful color change in the fall is why it is called Scarlet Oak.

T is for Tree,
seen near and far,
shining so bright;
way on top, a star.

Tt

Union Station opened on October 27, 1907. Back then, trains were the way to travel, even for presidents. In 1909, our 27th president, William Howard Taft, was the first to use the station. On April 14, 1945, a funeral train came to Union Station carrying the casket of our 32nd president, Franklin Delano Roosevelt. After Roosevelt's death, Vice President Harry Truman became our 33rd president.

Harry Truman and his wife, Bess were from Independence, Missouri. One of the most important decisions Harry Truman made while president was to use the atomic bomb on Japan during World War II. He was the first to desegregate the armed forces, to recognize the new state of Israel, and to help create the United Nations. When his term of office was over he went to Union Station and returned to Missouri by train. He spent his remaining days reading, writing, lecturing, and taking long brisk walks. He called himself "Mr. Citizen," and wrote a book using that title about his life after being president.

U is for Union Station.
President Truman and his wife
boarded a train for Missouri
to resume their former life.

V v

War memorials are moving tributes to the bravery and patriotism of the men and women who served our country in the armed forces. The World War II memorial is our newest war memorial and is located on the National Mall. It honors the 16 million who served in the armed forces during World War II including more than 400,000 who died and the millions who supported the war effort from home.

The African-American Civil War Memorial was unveiled on July 18, 1998. The bronze sculpture is 10 feet tall and features uniformed African-American soldiers and a sailor ready to leave home. Designer Ed Hamilton was the first African American to have a major piece of art to be placed on federal land anywhere in the District of Columbia.

The Vietnam Veterans Memorial, known as the Wall, is the most visited of all landmarks in our nation's capital.

Washington, D.C. is filled with memories of each and every war. V is for all Veterans who fought, wanting peace forevermore.

Our nation's capital official bird is the wood thrush, just over seven inches tall. Wood thrushes begin singing just before sunrise. They are famous for their beautiful flute-like voice that may combine two notes at one time. The males sometimes sing throughout the day but especially at dusk.

A special bird, although not a wood thrush, is on display in the National Museum of American History. It is a carrier pigeon named *Cher Ami*—French for "Dear Friend." It was one of 600 birds flown by the U.S. Army Signal Corps to deliver secret messages in France during World War I. On his last mission he was shot through the breast and leg by enemy fire. He still managed to reach home with his message capsule that helped save 200 men. He was awarded the French *Croix de Guerre* with Palm for his heroism and received a gold medal for his service to America.

W is for Wood Thrush
D.C.'s official bird.
Before the sun is up
its song is often heard.

W
W

X is for the X-1—
     it never went to the moon.
This plane is on display
     because of the sonic boom.

On October 14, 1947, the Bell X-1 became the first airplane to fly faster than the speed of sound. It was flown by U.S. Air Force Captain Charles E. "Chuck" Yeager. He reached a speed of 700 miles per hour at an altitude of 43,000 feet. It is on display in the Smithsonian Air and Space Museum in the Milestones of Flight gallery along with the Wright Brothers' 1903 flyer, Charles Lindbergh's *Spirit of St. Louis,* and many other famous aircraft. The Air and Space Museum is just one of the Smithsonian's 16 museums and is the most-visited. Nine of the Smithsonian museums are located on the National Mall.

James Smithson, a British scientist, drew up his last will and testament stipulating that, should his nephew die without heirs, the estate should go "to the United States of America, to found at Washington, under the name of the Smithsonian Institution, an establishment for the increase and diffusion of knowledge among men." His nephew did die without heirs and his fortune was sent to the United States. Nobody knows the reason for Smithson's decision. He never traveled to the United States and seems to have had no connection with anyone here.

X
X

Y is for the Yard—
a military base in D.C.
Can you guess which one?
They spend their time at sea.

In 1798 President John Adams appointed Benjamin Stoddert head of the newly established Department of the Navy. Stoddert started the Washington Navy Yard, the Navy's oldest shore establishment in 1799 located in our nation's capital. The Yard is on land set aside by George Washington for the federal government along the Anacostia River. It was an important defensive point during the War of 1812 and the Civil War.

The Yard has been used as a greeting place to our nation's capital. The first Japanese diplomatic mission was welcomed here in 1860. The body of World War I's Unknown Soldier was received at the Yard. Charles Lindbergh traveled on the USS *Memphis*, landing at the Yard after his famous transatlantic flight with the *Spirit of St. Louis* in 1927. The Yard is the port for the presidential yacht.

An Act of Congress in 1889 created our National Zoo. In 1890 it became part of the Smithsonian Institution. The Zoo is a 163-acre park set amid Rock Creek National Park in our nation's capital. It is home to more than 2,700 individual animals of 435 different species. Frederick Law Olmsted, a famous landscape architect, helped design the zoo to serve as a refuge for wildlife, such as bison and beaver, that were becoming extinct in North America.

Today the best-known residents are giant pandas, Tian Tian and Mei Xiang, currently on loan from the China Wildlife Conservation Association.

Z is for our National Zoo.
As this book comes to an end,
take time to visit our nation's capital
and bring along a friend!

Z z

A Capital Filled with Facts

1. Where did the Angel of the Battlefield work before the Civil War?

2. Where did President Truman live while the White House was being remodeled?

3. What is the difference between capitol and capital?

4. Who was our 16th president?

5. Which wing of the Capitol Building is home to the Senate?

6. Who was the commander of the Continental Army?

7. Who lives at 1600 Pennsylvania Avenue?

8. Who is the Teddy Bear named after?

9. Who wrote "The Stars and Stripes Forever"?

10. What are the names of the three buildings of the Library of Congress?

11. Who was first called the "first lady"?

12. Who started the Smithsonian Kite Festival?

13. Where did Sandra Day O'Connor grow up?

14. Who was Powhatan's daughter?

15. Who was the first family to live in the White House?

16. What are the two rivers that run through D.C.?

17. Who wrote "The Star-Spangled Banner"?

18. Who was the first president to light the national Christmas tree?

19. Who called himself Mr. Citizen?

20. What is the name of the bird that carried a message during WWI?

Answers

1. U.S. Patent Office
2. Blair House
3. Capitol is a building; Capital is a city
4. Abraham Lincoln
5. The north wing
6. George Washington
7. The president and his family
8. Theodore Roosevelt
9. John Philip Sousa
10. Thomas Jefferson, James Madison, and John Adams.
11. Dolley Madison
12. Paul E. Garber
13. On the Lazy B Ranch in Arizona
14. Pocahontas
15. The John Adams family
16. The Potomac and the Anacostia
17. Francis Scott Key
18. President Coolidge
19. President Truman, our 33rd president
20. Cher Ami

Marie and Roland Smith

N is for our Nation's Capital: A Washington, DC Alphabet is the fourth collaboration for Marie and Roland Smith. They also authored *Z is for Zookeeper: A Zoo Alphabet*, *B is for Beaver: An Oregon Alphabet* and *E is for Evergreen: A Washington Alphabet*. Roland is the author of many award-winning books for children including *Thunder Cave*, *Sasquatch*, *Jaguar*, *Zach's Lie*, and *The Captain's Dog: My Journey with the Lewis and Clark Tribe*.

Marie and Roland spend three to four months each year in the D.C. area. The remainder of the year is spent on their small farm south of Portland.

Barbara Leonard Gibson

Barbara Leonard Gibson received her B.F.A. from Carnegie Mellon University. She has illustrated more than three dozen books including *The Nutmeg Adventure*, *A Picture-Perfect World*, *Let's Explore a Tropical Forest*, *Hide & Seek*, the National Geographic Society's award-winning pop-up book, *Creatures of the Desert World*, and the six-book collection, *The Little Learner's Library I*. She also illustrated Patricia Cornwell's *Life's Little Fable* and more recently, best-selling children's author Audrey Penn's *The Whistling Tree* and *A Pocket Full of Kisses*.

An ardent environmentalist, she specializes in horse, wildlife, and nature illustration. When not engrossed in work, she can usually be found either at the small farm where her two horses are boarded, or at a therapeutic riding center where she volunteers her time. She and her composer husband, Robert, live in Olney, Maryland with their dog, Sadie. Their grown daughter, Caitlin, lives nearby.

American Idol

CELEBRATING 10 YEARS

THE OFFICIAL BACKSTAGE PASS

BY SHIRLEY HALPERIN

ABRAMS IMAGE, NEW YORK

FOREWORD *By Simon Fuller*

CREATOR AND EXECUTIVE PRODUCER, *AMERICAN IDOL*

It's rare that I get a moment to reflect. Usually, I'm either in the present or the future, and when I do look back on the past, I tend to think about things I would have done differently, rather than the glory of it. But ten years of *American Idol*—with its 55 million albums sold, 170 million songs downloaded, and nearly a billion votes cast—is certainly cause for celebration.

What drove me to launch *Idol* was simple: the desire to find new stars and the idea that the audience should have an equal part in the discovery process. The origin of *Idol* goes back to my days in England with the Spice Girls and S Club 7, where I was thinking about ways to use the Internet to audition thousands of people at a time. I pitched an idea that turned into a TV show, but it was missing an interactive element, and once I added that into the mix, *Pop Idol* was born.

At the time, the idea of an audience-voted competition show was revolutionary, but having been a manager and knowing how much hard work goes into making a great artist and finding that hit song, I was determined to prove that success can be achieved without taking the traditional route. The theory: If the public could choose the talent, it would be a self-fulfilling prophecy and the singer would be successful. The mechanism used was a recurring weekly showdown where we would end up with the best talent that already had a built-in audience and wouldn't be so dependent on radio. It turned out well, but the bigger success was the TV show.

Believe it or not, in the beginning, getting *Idol* on air in America was a nightmare. With our partners, Fremantle-Media, we had a miserable first-pitch trip, which resulted in total failure. Then the show launched in England where it was a huge success. We returned, and with the help of Creative Artists Agency (CAA), things went properly. Still, FOX was the only network that wanted it—all the others just didn't see past the mass auditions. Plus, *Idol* was so interactive and new that they didn't understand the power of that. But FOX president of alternative entertainment, Mike Darnell, did. He was a lone voice and, eventually, his enthusiasm would transcend the whole company.

What came next were the judges. Again, we tried to replicate the English format: two hosts and three judges. There was the bad guy—Simon Cowell—then we needed a girl's perspective and found Paula Abdul, who was quirky and a good foil for Simon. Randy Jackson was the moderate judge. It was such a powerful format that it worked not just in England and America, but also in more than fifty countries.

By and large, the American launch went brilliantly. The only thing that didn't work was the dynamic of having two hosts, so we had to address that. Ryan Seacrest excelled on his own, we could see that right away, and once we got to know him—his work ethic and how he handled himself on live television with such grace and professionalism—he became an instant phenomenon.

Of course, no one inspired more watercooler chatter than Simon. It's the nature of English people to be provocative generally; Americans are very polite, so the early seasons thrived on controversy. Simon played it up because it was getting reactions, but that form of criticism became one of the groundbreaking things about *Idol*: We pushed the boundaries of TV and headline news. People talked about *Idol* every week. It was relived throughout the media every day. It was all part of the fun and the analysis in getting to the heart of America. By the end of season one, we understood how this show worked, so that when it all came together in season two, I knew we had a blockbuster hit on our hands.

It all comes down to this: There's a different connection between an Idol and his or her fans. It's a much more intimate relationship. They feel like they know Kelly Clarkson or Carrie Underwood—it's a genuine love and fondness. This was the premise for the show and its stars beyond the stage or screen, and it carried over from season to season: When people identify with you and believe in your dream that they can help you realize, it's an embrace on a mass level that's unlike any other.

The show started strong with Kelly Clarkson, who's since become the most commercially successful Idol of all time, selling more than 23 million albums and 36 million singles, then had a great line-up of kids on season two. That year's finale between Ruben Studdard and Clay Aiken was a great showdown because it was really close and the results were shocking: It seemed Clay was a sure win, but America also fell in love with Ruben. That's the beauty of *Idol*: you never know which way it can go.

Season three had the brilliantly talented Fantasia, who had a rough life but was arguably the best singer we've ever had. America spotted her from the get-go, so much so that she outshined Jennifer Hudson. Both have done brilliantly, and I'm proud of that, but at the time, Fantasia was the one.

Season four was my favorite. It was a blockbuster year with Carrie Underwood and Bo Bice. Carrie, the perfect, all-American girl from a small town in Oklahoma—she's the true American dream, and the blueprint for what *American Idol* can do for a career.

Season five was a surprising year. I, along with millions of viewers, thought Chris Daughtry would walk away with that season, and it was a major shock when he left. But Taylor Hicks connected with America; he was different, charming, and a bit of an underdog. From that season on, we noticed that the contestants played up to the viewers more. They understood it was up to America—that the judges judge, but don't choose.

Season six brought Jordin Sparks, our youngest winner and a great singer and very sweet girl. It was a transitional year, which led to season seven, one of *Idol*'s most incredible line-ups. One hundred million votes were cast for David Cook and David Archuleta. And where Bo Bice started the notion that you could be a little different and Chris Daughtry pushed it more, David Cook drove it home. He has turned out to be a fantastic winner for *Idol*: thoughtful, insightful, true to himself, talented, and a real artist.

The next year, *Idol* had another classic showdown: Adam Lambert, who was outstanding, but polarized the audience—people either loved or hated him—and Kris Allen, who was such a nice guy, and America fell in love with him. I'm especially proud of this season because Adam has done well all over the world, and Kris singing Kanye West's "Heartless" was a true game-changing moment.

Season nine was another transitional year where we experimented. We tried changing the dynamic by adding Kara DioGuardi as the fourth judge and bringing in Ellen DeGeneres to replace Paula. But when you have such a strong character like Simon, it's hard to change the chemistry.

With season ten came refreshing, new ideas and two of the most qualified artists to take a seat at the judges' table. Jennifer Lopez felt like fate. She's the consummate professional: beautiful, confident, and funny, she identifies with the contestants, understands the industry, and has always loved the show. Randy has been there since season one and is a joy to work with, so we couldn't imagine him going anywhere. Then we needed a star who had earned his stripes, somebody legendary and extraordinary, and that was clearly Steven Tyler. He's eccentric, funny, knowledgable, and can be very sensitive, but he's also unpredictable and might say anything. Now, the energy is great, the spotlight is back on the contestants, Jimmy Iovine brings authority beyond what we've ever had before, and it's more real and less contrived on the panel.

Idol will be remembered for many things. The show embraced the digital age and grew with it—*Idol* was at the forefront of introducing texting to America, and the number of downloads we've sold on iTunes is incredible. And it produced a number of great artists who wouldn't have been found otherwise and will be remembered for many years. Imagine pop music without Kelly Clarkson and the world is a slightly drearier place. You could say the same for pop culture. Where would it be without *American Idol*?

INTRODUCTION *By Cecile Frot-Coutaz*

CEO, FREMANTLEMEDIA NORTH AMERICA; EXECUTIVE PRODUCER, *AMERICAN IDOL*

When you work on a program like *American Idol* and you're in the midst of the day-to-day production of the show, in some ways, you don't appreciate it as much as those on the outside. Then you exit the bubble, meet people, and instantly realize that everyone is watching and interested, and that *Idol* has become a phenomenon that's had an unprecedented impact on pop culture.

It took us some time to get to that place. During the first few years, we were always thinking, "It could end any day now." Even when the second season took off and the numbers were so extraordinary, everyone was thrilled, but nobody thought it could last—maybe two or three years and it would be over. It was only when we got to season three that we realized we would be around for a while, followed by five years where every season was bigger than the one before.

You can analyze the show to death, but its success comes down to one simple premise: it's the American dream, and people identify with it. The show is fundamentally about the contestants and their rise to stardom. It's partly a singing competition and partly a popularity contest, and that's why it's successful—because viewers relate with the contestants.

Of course, the judges are a big part of the equation. They became more prominent over the years because they turned into celebrities, but that panel also clicked like no other combination on television, which was another reason the show resonated so deeply with viewers. Randy Jackson brought credibility, good energy, and likability in spades— the exact opposite of Simon Cowell, whose thinking was always that Americans are too nice. He didn't care, and he told it like it was. Simon was something new and shocking, and during the first season, Paula Abdul was truly appalled to be sitting next to him. But you needed a foil, and that's what Paula was: a warm, encouraging personality who was sympathetic to everyone. To round out the group, we found Ryan Seacrest, who would end up part of a double hosting act, as we had in the UK, though we had originally debated whether to have him as a judge.

It became clear soon enough that the show was all about involvement—you need a great audience in the studio and captive viewers at home. You need good performances and some very bad ones. Action generates reaction from the judges, Ryan, and the audience. You want people to be surprised and the show to be unpredictable. You want things to go wrong sometimes.

It's been a great road and also a quite difficult one in other respects. What I'm most proud of is that this collective enterprise has kept the show going so long, given how many moving parts there are and different parties involved, including FremantleMedia, 19 Entertainment, the FOX network, the judges, and executive producers, Ken Warwick and Nigel Lythgoe. I'm proud of that. We've kept it running well throughout.

I'm also proud of *Idol*'s place as a platform for professional artists. Thinking back to one of the show's first guests, Lionel Richie, I remember his album sales went through the roof the day after his appearance. After Shakira and Wyclef Jean premiered "Hips Don't Lie" on *Idol*, it became an instant radio smash. From Alicia Keys to Gwen Stefani to Justin Bieber, Usher and Lady Gaga, the music business has come to realize that the show can boost a career.

Idol is now home to two highly credible artists, Jennifer Lopez and Steven Tyler, who we're lucky to have. You can't ask for better chemistry than the three judges from season ten. Randy brings the technical side, Steven is your wild unfiltered rock star, and Jennifer is a gorgeous role model to countless women and an accomplished actress and singer. They've all seen and seemingly done it all, but none have had the unique experience that is *American Idol*. It's been a lot of fun.

I'm very grateful to all the people who supported the show over the years, from all the crew to our partners and sponsors, and most importantly, the *Idol* fans. When I step back and survey how far we've come, I see America—this country that has embraced the show like no other, inspiring forty versions all over the world. That's something for which I am very proud.

1

CHAPTER 1: **IN THE BEGINNING . . .**

NO ONE QUITE KNEW WHAT TO EXPECT on June 11,

2002. That's the night a new FOX show called *American Idol* was beamed out to millions of households. It had a simple premise—a singing competition in which the viewers voted for their favorite contestant—and one lofty goal: "the search for a superstar." Thousands of wide-eyed auditioners would be whittled down to thirty-two finalists and, finally, one winner, who'd land a lucrative recording contract, a management deal, and be guaranteed a real shot at stardom. There to narrow the choices was a panel of three esteemed music business veterans, but in the end, America's eyes and ears did the judging, and they chose Kelly Clarkson.

When she arrived at the Dallas auditions in spring 2002, the cocktail waitress immediately stood out. She had the confidence of someone older than her twenty years, the pipes of a professional pop singer, and the looks to match. Plus she had sass, which Kelly put on full display her first time singing in front of the judges. Offering to switch places with Randy Jackson, she took a seat beside Paula Abdul while Randy went down on one knee and did his best R. Kelly. Later in the semifinals, Simon Cowell would famously declare that this incident was the only part of her audition that he could remember. Clearly, he had a bad memory.

Still, the competition was formidable. Season one boasted two tremendous soul singers, fourth-place finalist Tamyra Gray and Christina Christian, who was eliminated two weeks earlier. It also had a couple of edgy rockers, Ryan Starr and Nikki McKibbin, and a handful of boys who could run R&B circles around the best of amateurs. Chief among them, season one's runner-up Justin Guarini from Doylestown, Pennsylvania.

Walking us through the contest were two bubbly hosts, Ryan Seacrest and Brian Dunkleman—one, a savvy Dick Clark protégé, the other his comic foil. They followed each other's footsteps (literally, during the broadcast the two nearly always moved in unison), lent a shoulder to any contestant who needed one to cry on, and kept the mood upbeat and lively, despite having to send someone home every week. In the end, after fourteen performances—all of them unforgettable—only one escaped the bottom the whole way through and avoided hearing Seacrest deliver those fateful words. Instead, she heard these on finale night: "The winner of *American Idol* 2002 is . . . Kelly Clarkson."

CLASS *of*

02

SEASON 1 YEARBOOK

"You are a lady. You handle yourself with dignity and grace."
—Paula Abdul

CHRISTINA CHRISTIAN

"Singer/Songwriter"

SEASON 1

WINNER!

2002

KELLY CLARKSON

"Cocktail Waitress"

EJAY DAY

"Singer"

A. J. GIL

"High School Student"

TAMYRA GRAY

"Singer"

"You could be exactly what the American Idol is all about."
—Randy Jackson

"You were sensational."
—Simon Cowell

SEASON 1
RUNNER-UP
2002

JUSTIN GUARINI
"Amateur Theater Director-Singer"

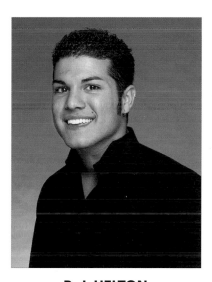

R. J. HELTON
"Singer"

NIKKI MCKIBBIN
"Singer"

RYAN STARR
"Singer"

JIM VERRAROS
"Student"

KELLY CLARKSON

* **HOMETOWN:** Burleson, Texas

* **AUDITION SONG:** "Express Yourself" by Madonna

* **WORDS TO LIVE BY:** *"I'm so pleased that you've entered this show, and you're gonna do so well. I truly, truly believe you are gonna become a huge star after this show."* —Simon

* **LIFE AFTER *IDOL*:** Kelly Clarkson wasted no time making—and breaking—records soon after the competition ended. Her debut single, the coronation song "A Moment Like This," was a hit straight out of the gate, selling more than 236,000 copies in its first week out in October 2002. Six months later, her full-length album *Thankful* also topped the *Billboard* charts and spawned the radio smash "Miss Independent." The girl-power anthem (written by Christina Aguilera) spent five weeks in the number one spot and showed that Kelly's was a voice to be reckoned with.

But proving there was a bona fide musical powerhouse behind those insane pipes was Kelly's sophomore CD, 2004's *Breakaway*, which sold more than 6 million copies and launched no fewer than five hit singles, including the instant classic "Since U Been Gone" and the ballad "Because of You," which Kelly wrote when she was sixteen years old as a way to cope with her parents' divorce. National TV appearances followed, including much-coveted bookings on *Saturday Night Live* and *The Oprah Winfrey Show*, along with a slew of awards, among them Grammys for Best Pop Vocal Performance and Best Pop Vocal Album.

With several international tours in between, and music legends of all genres—from Reba McEntire to Melissa Etheridge—doubling as her duet partners, there was no stopping Kelly Clarkson's meteoric rise to pop stardom, which continued with 2007's *My December*, a darker album she largely wrote herself, and 2009's *All I Ever Wanted*, a return to form that had Kelly belting "My Life Would Suck Without You." Now that she's approaching her own ten-year

American Idol anniversary, perhaps we should be directing that same sentiment toward Kelly.

JUSTIN GUARINI

❊ **HOMETOWN:** Doylestown, Pennsylvania

❊ **AUDITION SONGS:** "Who's Loving You" by Smokey Robinson; "Blame It on the Sun" by Stevie Wonder

❊ **WORDS TO LIVE BY:** *"You have that* American Idol *thing going on, dude. Wow."* —Randy

❊ **LIFE AFTER *IDOL*:** Long after his season one run, Justin Guarini remains among *Idol*'s most recognized alum—and not just because of his hair! Though he finished second, Justin was also signed to a major label recording contract and released his self-titled debut in June 2003. The album, which showcased Justin's soulful vocals over a modern-day funk-influenced sound, coincided with the movie *From Justin to Kelly*, after which he took his velvety-smooth voice to a new stage as cohost of TV Guide Channel's *Idol Wrap* and *Idol Tonight* shows and a regular on the red carpet. While he is a man of many talents, music remains closest to Justin's heart, no matter what the genre. Case in point: his self-produced 2005 album, *Stranger Things Have Happened*, which features reinterpretations of jazz classics. But four years later, he was squeezing into a pair of cowboy boots for the CMT show *Gone Country*, which begs the question: Where will this versatile performer go next?

NIKKI MCKIBBIN

❊ **HOMETOWN:** Grand Prairie, Texas

❊ **AUDITION SONGS:** "I Will Survive" by Gloria Gaynor; "One Moment in Time" by Whitney Houston

❊ **WORDS TO LIVE BY:** *"You have originality, you're doing your own thing, and I think this is what this competition should be about, finding somebody more unique with an individual style and a talent and I hope you do really well in this competition because I think you deserve to."* —Simon

❊ **LIFE AFTER *IDOL*:** Nikki McKibbin earned the nickname Comeback Kid during her *Idol* tenure, having landed in the bottom three during all but one week—six times in total! That resilience carried her through some trying times following her third-place elimination. A year after releasing her debut album, 2007's dark, hard-driving rocker *Unleashed*, Nikki checked into VH1's *Celebrity Rehab with Dr. Drew*, then

Sober House in 2009, to confront her addiction demons. It was there that she penned and performed the song "Inconsolable," an ode to her own recovery.

TAMYRA GRAY

* **HOMETOWN:** Norcross, Georgia

* **AUDITION SONG:** "Treated Me Kind" by Mariah Carey

* **WORDS TO LIVE BY:** *"Whitney Houston, Celine Dion, Mariah Carey, move on over, here comes Tamyra!"* —Paula

* **LIFE AFTER *IDOL*:** An H&M ad campaign and acting roles on Broadway (*Rent*), in film (*The Gospel*), and on TV (*Boston Public*) kept former Miss Atlanta Tamyra Gray in the public eye, while in her private life, she married Color Me Badd singer Sam Watters, who produced her debut album, *The Dreamer*, in 2006.

R. J. HELTON

* **HOMETOWN:** Cumming, Georgia

* **AUDITION SONG:** "Never Can Say Goodbye" by The Jackson 5

* **WORDS TO LIVE BY:** *"I want you to know, R.J., I love you more than your initials, and in this business where most people fly coach, you fly first-class."* —Paula

* **LIFE AFTER *IDOL*:** After bowing out in fifth place, R. J. Helton caught the eye of Matthew Knowles (manager and father of Beyoncé), who helped the silky-voiced crooner release 2004's *Real Life*. Showcasing R.J.'s brand of Latin-influenced pop soul, the album landed in the top twenty of *Billboard*'s Christian charts

and garnered a Dove Award nomination. A year later, R.J. moved to Louisiana, where Hurricane Katrina set him on a new path: charity work. R.J. currently resides in San Francisco, where he continues to inspire people with his music and generosity of spirit.

CHRISTINA CHRISTIAN

* **HOMETOWN:** Pembroke Pines, Florida

* **AUDITION SONG:** "At Last" by Glenn Miller

* **WORDS TO LIVE BY:** *"OK, I admit it, I've got a crush."* —Simon

* **LIFE AFTER *IDOL*:** The stunning Christina Christian may have been Simon Cowell's season one crush, but after her week-four elimination (which she missed due to illness—an *Idol* first), she returned to her home state of Florida and won the heart of Nicholas Cewe, whom she married in 2004. Now a mom and a businesswoman, Christina Christian still works toward a career as a singer-songwriter.

RYAN STARR

* **HOMETOWN:** Sunland, California

* **AUDITION SONGS:** "Lean on Me" by Bill Withers; "Falling" by Alicia Keys

* **WORDS TO LIVE BY:** *"You look like a star, sound like a star, perform like a star."* —Randy

* **LIFE AFTER *IDOL*:** Ryan Starr was a natural in front of the camera, so it's no wonder she continued her residency on the small screen, making an appearance on *That '70s Show* soon after singing her last note during 1970s Week, then joining the cast of VH1's *The Surreal Life* in 2004, among other TV gigs. But music—and Ryan's signature style—never took a backseat, and her

debut single, "My Religion," an exclusive iTunes release, was among the digital retailer's early hits, selling a whopping 360,000 downloads.

A. J. GIL

* **HOMETOWN:** San Diego, California

* **AUDITION SONG:** The National Anthem

* **WORDS TO LIVE BY:** *"You have one of those real nice, pure voices that when you hit it right and you get into the groove of the song, you really shine."* —Paula

* **LIFE AFTER *IDOL*:** The *American Idol* experience illuminated A. J. Gil's true calling, which was to continue working in the music business. After finishing eighth on season one, the R&B crooner who oozed Latin flavor took a few years off to hone his skills, both in front of the microphone and behind the scenes as an audio engineer. His latest mixtape, "Love Me Later," was released in July 2010.

JIM VERRAROS

* **HOMETOWN:** Crystal Lake, Illinois

* **AUDITION SONG:** "When I Fall in Love" by Nat King Cole

* **WORDS TO LIVE BY:** *"Both my parents are deaf… It's kind of sad since I've been a singer for so long and my parents will never be able to hear me sing."* —Jim Verraros

* **LIFE AFTER *IDOL*:** While being the second contestant voted off *Idol*'s first top ten doesn't necessarily bode well for a successful music career, Jim Verraros beat the odds by landing a major recording contract with Koch Records and scoring a top twenty dance hit with the sultry "You Turn It On" off his 2005 debut, *Rollercoaster*. Indeed, it had been one rocky ride for the musical talent born to deaf parents, which included Jim's "coming out" to *The Advocate* in 2003, but in the end, he found professional achievement as an actor in the DVD series *Eating Out* and personal triumph in marrying longtime love Bill Brennan in 2009.

EJAY DAY

* **HOMETOWN:** Lawrenceville, Georgia

* **AUDITION SONG:** "I'll Be" by Edwin MCain

* **WORDS TO LIVE BY:** *"Each time I walk on that stage, I say to myself, knock them dead or don't knock them at all…."* —EJay Day

* **LIFE AFTER *IDOL*:** EJay Day was a last-minute replacement who survived only two rounds on America's premier singing competition, but that didn't hamper the aspiring performer from pursuing his dreams. After writing a track that appeared on Raven-Symoné's *Unstoppable* album, EJay released his own music, the funky "Come into My World," to coincide with touring appearances across the United States and on the great wide sea.

Greatest Hits

LATELY

R. J. HELTON

JULY 2, 2002

It was sink or swim during the wild-card round. Only one of five was going through, and that spot was awarded to the silky-smooth R. J. Helton, who impressed the judges with his pitch-perfect vocals on the Stevie Wonder ballad.

FOR ONCE IN MY LIFE

JUSTIN GUARINI

JULY 16, 2002

The performance that introduced Justin Guarini to *American Idol*'s first top ten was one minute and twenty seconds' worth of booty-shaking grooves and endlessly flirtatious moves that bowled Paula over—literally! Simon was impressed as well, comparing the instant contender's Motown Week bow to another Justin: Timberlake.

(YOU MAKE ME FEEL LIKE) A NATURAL WOMAN

KELLY CLARKSON

JULY 23, 2002

Kelly Clarkson had already gained the R.E.S.P.E.C.T. of judges and audience alike during the semifinals when she belted an Aretha Franklin classic with the vocal prowess of a singer far beyond her years, but it was her 1960s Week rendition of this soulful love song that put her in a league of her own with the *Idol* crown in sight. Said Paula: "You truly are amazing."

AIN'T NO SUNSHINE

CHRISTINA CHRISTIAN

JULY 30, 2002

Channeling chanteuse Sade in style and sound, Christina Christian delivered a confident, nuanced performance of the Bill Withers classic during 1970s Night—a marked improvement from the previous week, which prompted Simon to remark, "I think you've absolutely found your niche," and Paula to declare, "If this were the Olympics, this would be your golden moment."

A HOUSE IS NOT A HOME

TAMYRA GRAY

AUGUST 13, 2002

With her inner diva on full display, Tamyra Gray hit this Burt Bacharach tune out of the park during Love Songs Week. "That performance was on a par with Whitney Houston, Celine Dion," said Simon. "It was one of the best I've ever seen on TV."

BLACK VELVET

NIKKI MCKIBBIN

AUGUST 27, 2002

Proving her rock might for a seventh straight week, Nikki McKibbin's finest hour on the *Idol* stage would turn out to be her last. Still, the bluesy Alannah Myles hit, the judges' choice on Top Three Week, showcased her gritty vocals and undeniable raw talent, which Randy declared her "best song yet."

CHAPTER 2: **SIMON COWELL**

SIMON COWELL 101

Somewhere between Richard Branson, David Geffen, and Donald Trump sits Simon Cowell, England's most-talked-about export since The Beatles hit the charts in 1962. As the snippy senior judge of America's most popular talent contest for nine straight years, Simon elicits shrieks along with a healthy dose of boos and gasps. Still, he has a certain charm, which keeps us all coming back for more, and as infuriating as his comments can be, more often than not, they're right.

Of course, it wasn't always so. With every great success story usually comes a series of stumbles, and Simon Cowell's is no exception. His music business career started at the bottom of the ladder, the mail room at EMI Music Publishing, from where he slowly climbed the ranks until he was able to make a move to BMG and soon break away and form his own company, the first of many. But even after scoring a handful of hits, economic realities and a heavy debt load forced a thirty-year-old Simon to move back into his parents' house in 1989.

Taking time to assess his situation, Simon and his S-Records emerged even stronger than before, churning out a string of qualified smashes. A little more than a decade later, Simon created Syco Music, which later became a subsidiary of the recording giant Sony Music, releasing albums by international superstars Il Divo and Westlife.

It was around this time in 2001 that television came into Simon's world in the form of the show *Pop Idol*. The British predecessor to *American Idol* became an instant phenomenon and its winner a bona fide star, green-lighting its U.S. adaptation in due haste. What followed were nine seasons of jeers, insults, and the occasional compliment, yet we loved every minute of it. And so did our cousins from across the pond, who seem to have unilaterally endorsed his judgeship on multiple programs, including *Britain's Got Talent*, the show that made Susan Boyle a YouTube sensation and household name, and *The X Factor*, which discovered Leona Lewis. Season nine marked Simon's last with the *Idol* franchise, but he's still knee-deep in the talent pool, searching near and far for the next big hit.

MAN OF MANY WORDS, FEW SHIRTS

Simon Cowell is not one for drastic change. Look no further than his haircut and T-shirt collection. Still, there was the occasional veering away from his stagnant style. Here, Simon's twists on his limited tops.

AFTERNOON TEE: Simon's go-to T-shirt was tight and black, becoming one of his best known looks.

COWELL CLEAVAGE: When Simon wasn't showing off his toned muscles, his tan took center stage, in the form of a blindingly white collared shirt, buttoned down to the ab line.

SUITED FOR GOOD: To illustrate the seriousness of the Idol Gives Back charity initiatives, Simon would suit up in his favorite brand, Armani—sans tie, of course (see left), but dashing nonetheless.

TIGHTY WHITEY: Simon mainstay is the skin-hugging white V-neck T-shirt, which may look like your standard undershirt, but we're sure cost nearly six times as much!

SWEATER CHEST: In the often frigid *Idol* studio, Simon would sometimes sport one of several black sweaters— all of them tight—giving new meaning to the term turning up the heat.

GRAY MATTERS: Simon must have owned hundreds of gray crew necks, the shirt that made the most repeat appearances on *Idol*.

SIMON'S ONE-LINERS

> "I thought the first part of the song was hideous. It was like a sleeping pill... awful."
> —to Mikalah Gordon (SEASON FOUR)

A COLLECTION OF THE "BEST ZINGERS" IN THE COWELL CANON.

> "I think thirty million TV sets in American had their volume turned down simultaneously during that song." —to Lindsey Cardinale (SEASON FOUR)

> "If you win this competition, we will have failed."
> —to Jim Verraros (SEASON ONE)

> "It was akin to the office Christmas party where somebody attempts at the end of the evening to get up and entertain everybody else and they fail." —to Anthony Federov (SEASON FOUR)

> "If you lived two thousand years ago and sang like that, they would've stoned you." —to Chris West (SEASON TWO)

> "Hideous. Everything about that was horrible." —to Anthony Federov (SEASON FOUR)

> "Let me just put this into perspective. If you were to win and sing a song, you would kill the Amercan record industry. That's how bad you are. I don't wanna be rude but you could be the worst singer in New York."
> —to Christopher Boehm (SEASON TWO)

> "That was the equivalent of musical wallpaper... In other words, you notice the wallpaper, but you don't remember it."
> —to Nadia Turner (SEASON FOUR)

> "You are a beautiful girl, but you're ugly when you perform." —to Heather Piccinini (SEASON THREE)

> "I'd pack your suitcase tonight." —to Scott Savol (SEASON FOUR)

> "It was like dinner with Paula Abdul: sweet but forgettable."
> —to Jasmine Trias (SEASON THREE)

> "Let me use a horoscope analogy . . . you and your suitcase will be on a plane within twenty-four hours."
> —to Janay Castine (SEASON FOUR)

> "The problem is the horrible, cutesy routine you do with your songs." —to Diana DeGarmo (SEASON THREE)

> "It would be rather like ordering a guard dog for your home and getting delivered a poodle in a leather jacket. It's not the real thing." —to Constantine Maroulis, (SEASON FOUR)

> "You single-handedly could kill the music video industry. That was definitely a radio performance." —to Taylor Hicks (SEASON FIVE)

"That was a terrible imper-sonation of Elvis Presley. The dancing was hideous. It was just karaoke with a capital K."

—to Taylor Hicks (SEASON FIVE)

"I think you murdered the arrangement. You turned a beautiful song into a complete and utter drone." —to Chris Sligh (SEASON SIX)

"There were moments of complete torture in that vocal." —to Sanjaya (SEASON SIX)

"I think it had all the joy of someone singing at a funeral parlor. It was completely and utterly gloomy and slightly dark."

—to Phil Stacey (SEASON SIX)

"That was utterly horrendous. It was as bad as any-thing we've seen at the beginning of American Idol. This was funny for a while, but now it's ridiculous. Based on the fact that we're trying to find the next American Idol, this is horrendous." —to Sanjaya Malakar (SEASON SIX)

"The look is like something out of the Addams Family. The singing was out of control, ranging on shrieking. It was terrible." —to Jordin Sparks (SEASON SIX)

"You sounded like Dolly Parton on helium."

—to Kristy Lee Cook (SEASON SEVEN)

"I thought it was corny verging on desperate." —to David Hernandez (SEASON SEVEN)

"It was like ordering a hamburger and getting only the buns." —to Brooke White (SEASON SEVEN)

"I think you may have just blown a massive opportunity by being forget-table." —to Brent Keith (SEASON EIGHT)

"I thought it was verging on terrible. You were like a windup doll that never stopped smiling throughout the song." —to Haeley Vaughn (SEASON NINE)

"There's a certain irony for you singing a song about climbing when you actually fell off." —to Haeley Vaughn (SEASON NINE)

"There was a certain irony to you screech-ing out 'You're no good, you're no good, you're no good' over and over again . . . "

—to Didi Benami (SEASON NINE)

"If you listen to one of those dancing shows, they always have the singer murdering the song on it. That's what it kind of . . . " —to Didi Benami (SEASON NINE)

"The problem was the arrangement was horrific. You sucked the soul out of that song. Sucked it out and tortured it and ruined one of the greatest pop songs of all time. And at the same time, you made yourself really, really corny." —to Andrew Garcia (SEASON NINE)

SIMON'S ALWAYS RIGHT

While he never leaped out of his seat screaming "Told you so!" there's no doubt Simon Cowell has taken great pleasure in seeing some of his on-air predictions come true. Here, five examples of Simon comments that were particularly spot-on.

RUBEN STUDDARD

Can Simon see into the future? Even in the top twenty-four stage of season two, he pointed to early performances by Ruben Studdard ("Superstar") and Clay Aiken ("Open Arms") as signs of a potential finale showdown. "We're gonna have two dimensions to this competition this year," he explained on week two of the semifinals, "vocals over image."

Disco Week brought out the best of Ruben Studdard's velvety moves when he took on Barry White's smooth "Can't Get Enough of Your Love, Babe." It was only the third round of the top twelve, but the performance prompted Simon to expound, "Working for a record label, you try to separate good singers from future stars—I think you should win this competition."

FANTASIA BARRINO

Way back in season three's top thirty-two, Simon had already taken notice of the single mom from North Carolina with the otherworldly voice, telling Fantasia, "You're destined to be a star." Sure enough, twelve weeks and eighteen performances later, she was the last contestant standing and sewed up her win with a roof-raising rendition of 2004's coronation song, "I Believe," which seemed as if it were written just for her. "That was your acceptance speech," Simon declared. "Congratulations."

CARRIE UNDERWOOD

She had just made the top eleven, and for that week's theme, *Billboard* number one hits, Carrie chose a rocker: Heart's "Alone." The powerhouse performance left the *Idol* studio flabbergasted, especially Simon, who proclaimed, "You're not just the girl to beat, you're the person to beat." As it turned out, Simon spoke the truth. "I will make a prediction," he continued. "Not only will you win this show, you will sell more records than any other previous *Idol* winner."

DAVID ARCHULETA

It was the start of the top twenty-four and Simon had just criticized David Archuleta's choice of a "gloomy" song (Phil Collins's "Another Day in Paradise") for the second week in a row, telling him, "You've gotta lighten up a little bit." But that's not to say Simon didn't appreciate the immense talent standing before him. "There's no question you'll make it through to the finals next week," he said, calming the Archie devotees in the audience. "You're probably going to be in the final two." Correct again.

LEE DEWYZE

It had only been a couple weeks since America was introduced to the sheepish Lee DeWyze, but *Idol*'s head judge saw something special in the former paint boy's throaty take on Hinder's "Lips of an Angel." Said Simon, "I'm just waiting for you to totally connect, lose your nerves, choose the right song, sing as good as we know you can, [and] you may be the one to beat."

Simon is always RIGHT!

SINGING SIMON'S PRAISES

At the end of season nine, Simon Cowell decided to leave *American Idol*, and many thought the show would never be the same without him. *"I've had the best ten years of my life. I really mean this, thank you, and I'll miss you,"* he said on the season nine finale. *"Somebody once told me, 'you've gotta know when to leave the party.' It's simple as that. Genuinely, I can walk away with happy memories."*

Simon's unfiltered on-air cracks made headlines, but how did it feel to be on the receiving end of his criticism? *Idol* alumni, mentors, and fellow judges chime in on the positive side of Mr. Nasty.

ACE YOUNG

"Simon is a big reason why people watch the show—you never know what he's going to say, but he says what a lot of people are thinking. As a contestant, you've gotta be able to take the criticism."

PAULA ABDUL

"My darling Simon, I've worked with a lot of people over the years . . . hot cheerleaders, big movie stars, world-famous recording artists, even a cartoon cat. If I'm being truly honest, none of them holds a candle to you, my friend."

DAVID ARCHULETA

"People put their trust in Simon. They've built their foundation on whatever Simon says. Even if they like something, they'll change their mind if he says it's terrible. And vice versa. Simon has a strong influence on people."

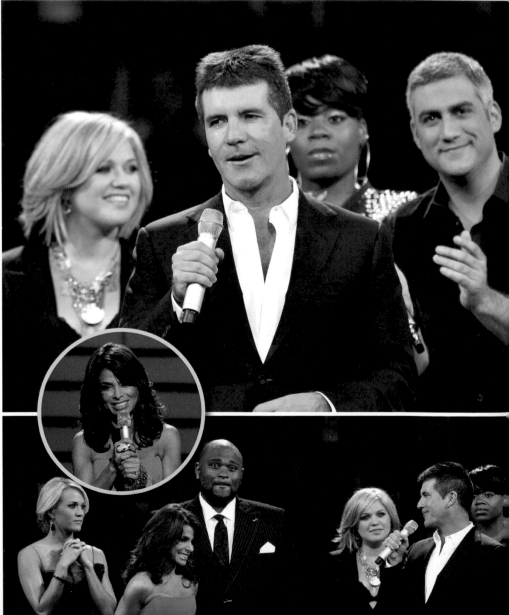

FANTASIA

"I think that the show will be very very different without you. You bring a lot to American Idol, so you will be missed. I would like to say thank you, from the bottom of my heart, for everything you said to me. Everything wasn't always good, but it was needed. I took it and I ran with it, and I love you to death. You're so fine—I've always wanted to tell you that."

RANDY JACKSON

"Simon has some of the best intuition in the game—he learns, he listens, he studies, he's not afraid in this time when everyone is copycatting everything to death. He's one of the most talented people I know."

KELLY CLARKSON

"Simon is a sexy man, but the difference is, Simon knows he's a sexy man."

LEE DEWYZE

"Simon is actually a really cool dude. It's his job to get up there and tell us what he thinks."

DAVID FOSTER

"The great thing about Simon is that he's musically knowledgeable and almost everything he says on the show is right. Like everybody else, I tune in to see what he says. It's what we professionals would like to say if there wasn't such a thing as dancing around the truth."

RYAN SEACREST

"Simon is a very clever and enterprising personality who has a really good gut. Sometimes I like to call him for his opinion. Believe it or not, we give each other genuine advice."

KARA DIOGUARDI

"I'm gonna miss him because I learned a lot from him. It's been fun sitting next to him, now that he doesn't roll his eyes at me, because that wasn't fun."

CRYSTAL BOWERSOX

"Simon, I know you're a tough guy. You say it like you mean it and I love that about you."

3

MERE WEEKS AFTER KELLY CLARKSON was crowned the first-ever American Idol, the show's audition team was back up and running. Tryouts for season two were held in six cities during the fall of 2002, and thanks to the runaway success of the show's debut, the production was able to afford a few perks: a backdrop, for one, and a glass desk, a step up from the logo-adorned glorified lunch table of year one. There were more significant changes as well: Gone was Brian Dunkleman, while Ryan Seacrest remained to handle all hosting duties solo; rather than a top ten, the last leg of the competition was expanded to twelve finalists; and guest judges were introduced, allowing the contestants a chance to interact with music legends from multiple genres and eras, among them Smokey Robinson, Olivia Newton-John, Lionel Richie, and Neil Sedaka.

Curiously, two of the top five finalists almost didn't make the cut at all. North Carolina crooner Clay Aiken and Memphis soul sister Trenyce were both wild card picks—the former voted through by the public, the latter by Paula Abdul—who narrowly made it through to the top twelve. Also advancing was seventeen-year-old Carmen Rasmusen, Simon Cowell's choice, and Kimberly Caldwell, Randy Jackson's pick and a rocker with some serious grit. Seven others vied for the title, including Kimberley Locke and Josh Gracin, a Marine with the country pipes to match his military-bred brawn. But the front-runner straight out the gate was undoubtedly Ruben Studdard. Dubbed "the Velvet Teddy Bear" by soul diva Gladys Knight, the undiscovered talent from Birmingham, Alabama was an R&B powerhouse who never missed a note and needed only ninety seconds to bring the house down.

You could say the same of his counterpart Clay, who exhibited the kind of confidence a lifelong entertainer spends years building, not what you'd expect from a special education student who'd never been onstage. Indeed, Clay was full of surprises, not the least of which involved a complete style transformation from geek to chic.

The final showdown at the Gibson Ampitheatre in Los Angeles was a night of standing ovations for both, and in the end, only 134,000 votes out of 24 million separated the winner, Ruben, from his runner-up, Clay, a result that, in the hearts of countless Claymates, remains as hotly debated today as it was on the night of May 21, 2003.

CLASS *of*
03

SEASON 2 YEARBOOK

SEASON 2
RUNNER-UP
2003

CLAY AIKEN

"College Student"

KIMBERLY CALDWELL

"Personal Assistant"

COREY CLARK

"Stage Hand"

JULIA DEMATO

"Hairdresser"

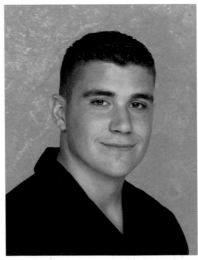

JOSH GRACIN

"Marine"

CHARLES GRIGSBY

"Supermarket Clerk"

"Look out, Garth Brooks, the Marines have landed."
—Lionel Richie

"You are ear-delicious."
—Neil Sedaka

KIMBERLEY LOCKE
"Student"

VANESSA OLIVAREZ
"Hair Colorist"

CARMEN RASMUSEN
"High School Student"

RICKEY SMITH
"College Student"

SEASON 2
WINNER!
2003

RUBEN STUDDARD
"College Student"

TRENYCE
"Retail Manager"

"You were definitely born to be a singer." —Randy Jackson

Looking back with the season two champ

What inspired you to audition for *Idol*?

Ruben Studdard: I didn't really plan on auditioning for the show; one of my friends wanted to try out, so I went with her to be one of those people outside holding the signs. And that day, when we were sleeping outside, something in me, I know it was God, was telling me, "Yo, man, this could be your shot." So I auditioned and I made it.

How did you choose your songs?

RS: People would wait a day or so to pick their song, but I would always go through the list and pick that very same day. That way, I could spend time on it and give a great performance. I would pick the songs I knew. There was only one week when I had to choose something that I wasn't comfortable with and that was when Diane Warren was there.

How did it feel to be in front of the judges the first time?

RS: It was a wonderful experience. I did Stevie Wonder's "Ribbon in the Sky." I actually sang it at the audition prior for Nigel [Lythgoe] and since I did so well with him, I sang it again. I still remember to this day—I was wearing my brother's sweater and his gold chain. I never thought in my wildest dreams that I would be getting ready to go to Hollywood but that's what God planned for me.

How did you feel about the nickname Gladys Knight gave you, the "Velvet Teddy Bear?"

RS: I loved it! It's stuck with me for a while and I still love it.

What did you think your chances were of making it to the final two?

RS: Honestly, it was so much fun being on the show that I never concerned myself with whether I was going to win or not. I'd never been to Los Angeles or lived in a mansion—everything was so new to me. I think that's why I was able to be so calm the whole time because I never really concerned myself with being American Idol. I was just there to enjoy the experience.

RUBEN STUDDARD

✳ **HOMETOWN:** Birmingham, Alabama

✳ **AUDITION SONG:** "Ribbon in the Sky" by Stevie Wonder

✳ **WORDS TO LIVE BY:** *"You are and will probably someday be the world's velvet teddy bear. You are awesome. Your voice just strokes the spirit."* —Gladys Knight

✳ **LIFE AFTER *IDOL*:** He had a big voice and when it came time for season two champ Ruben Studdard to release his debut single, a cover of Westlife's "Flying Without Wings," it also hit big, landing at number two on the *Billboard* Hot 100. Six months later, Ruben's album *Soulful* topped the album charts, selling more than 400,000 copies in its first week and garnering a Grammy nomination for the song "Superstar."

Three more full-length efforts followed 2004's *I Need an Angel*, 2006's *Return,* and 2009's *Love Is*, along with a "best of" in 2010, but Ruben also dove into acting, appearing on several TV shows, including *8 Simple Rules* and *Eve*, and later landing a starring role as Fats Waller in the stage revival of *Ain't Misbehavin'*. The national touring production, which also featured fellow finalist Trenyce and season one auditioner Frenchie Davis, brought Ruben his second Grammy nod, this time for Best Musical Show Album.

But while Ruben has gained in music business stature, he's lost more than a few inches around the waist—approximately eighty pounds, to be exact—as part of a vegan diet. He revealed his slimmer look on the *Idol* stage during season nine, using the opportunity to announce an encore tour with Clay Aiken.

Always keeping his community as a top priority, Ruben has set up a foundation aimed at promoting the arts to youngsters in and around Birmingham. He's also the spokesperson for Be Sickle Smart, a campaign to raise awareness of sickle-cell disease. Now, about that big heart . . .

CLAY AIKEN

❋ **HOMETOWN:** Raleigh, North Carolina

❋ **AUDITION SONG:** "Always and Forever" by Heatwave

❋ **WORDS TO LIVE BY:** *"I think the fact that you don't look like a traditional pop star is actually a good thing because you're so memorable."* —Simon

❋ **LIFE AFTER *IDOL*:** Clay Aiken may have been 134,000 votes shy of the win, but season two's runner-up is among *Idol*'s most successful alums, having sold upward of six million albums in the seven years since he stole America's heart. In fact, Clay's career began at the top of the charts. His debut album for the RCA label, 2003's *Measure of a Man*, featuring the radio smash "Invisible," landed at the number one spot its first week out, moving 613,000 copies.

The following Christmas was extra-special for Claymates everywhere, as their favorite Idol released the 2004 collection *Merry Christmas with Love* and starred in his own NBC holiday special, which Clay also executive produced. It would be the first of many television appearances for the wild-card-pick–turned–pop-star, who played small parts in shows like *Scrubs* and *Ed* before landing a costarring role in Broadway's *Spamalot* in 2008. In between, he recorded two more albums, toured tirelessly, and released a best-selling book, *Learning to Sing: Hearing the Music in Your Life*.

But perhaps the most eye-grabbing headlines concerned Clay's private life, namely, a September 2008 *People* magazine cover story in which he revealed that he was gay. Since then, Clay has added another album, 2010's *Tried and True,* to his extensive résumé, along with a new title: father. His son, Parker, was born in 2008.

Long recognized for his out-of-this-world voice, Clay Aiken is equally admired for his charity work. Be it his role as a national ambassador to UNICEF, which has sent him to tsunami-ravaged Bandeh Aceh, Mexico, Somalia, Kenya, and Afghanistan, or as an advocate for children with physical and mental disabilities, Clay's passion lies in helping others. He can't help himself.

der" and "Wrong," from her Curb Records debut, *One Love*. By the time her second album, 2007's *Based on a True Story*, came out, Kimberley had fully embraced her *Idol* alter ego K-Lo—and a dance music superstar was born. Two years later, she signed with Randy Jackson's Dream Merchant 21 label, releasing the funky single "Strobelight" in April 2010.

JOSH GRACIN

❋ **HOMETOWN:** Oceanside, California

❋ **AUDITION SONG:** "All or Nothing" by Cher

❋ **WORDS TO LIVE BY:** *"You've got this great country folk quality to your voice and you shine. You are who you are, there's no BS about you. Great job."* —Paula

❋ **LIFE AFTER *IDOL*:** Lance Corporal Josh Gracin had to forgo the *Idol* summer tour so that he could return to active duty in the U.S. Marine Corps, but within months of his honorable discharge in 2004, the top four finalist had moved to Nashville and signed a recording contract with Lyric Street Records, releasing his self-titled country debut in June of that year. The album yielded three singles, all of which reached the top five on the country charts, and was certified gold in 2005. Its out-of-the-gate success paved the way for a second studio effort, 2008's *We Weren't Crazy,* and in 2010 Josh released a fan appreciation EP for free to coincide with a nationwide tour. When he's not rocking his burly self onstage, Josh is dad to three daughters and husband to longtime love, Ann Marie.

KIMBERLEY LOCKE

❋ **HOMETOWN:** Gallatin, Tennessee

❋ **AUDITION SONG:** "Somewhere Over the Rainbow" by Judy Garland

❋ **WORDS TO LIVE BY:** *"As they say in the 'hood, where I grew up: you can saaang."* —Smokey Robinson

❋ **LIFE AFTER IDOL:** Following her top three showing, Kimberley Locke expanded her post-*Idol* portfolio to include a modeling contract (with Ford Models' full-figured division) and a stint on VH1's *Celebrity Fit Club*, after which she lost more than forty pounds. When it came to music, she was no less ambitious, releasing two top forty singles in 2004, "8th World Won-

TRENYCE

❋ **HOMETOWN:** Memphis, Tennessee

❋ **AUDITION SONG:** "Ribbon in the Sky" by Stevie Wonder

❋ **WORDS TO LIVE BY:** *"You're either born with it or you're not. You are born with it, you remind me of a brand-new fresh Diana Ross. You were my wild card pick and I can't imagine this competition without you."* —Paula

❋ **LIFE AFTER *IDOL*:** After appearing on the *Idol* summer tour, fifth-place finisher Trenyce realized her true calling: the theater. Honing her acting chops in stage productions of *Dreamgirls*, *The Vagina Monologues*, *Soul Kittens Cabaret,* and *Love in the Nick of Tyme*, Trenyce shared the spotlight with veteran actresses like Vanessa Williams, Tatyana Ali, and Jackée Harry. But *Idol* was never far from her heart, and she later reunited with season two winner Ruben Studdard and season one contender Frenchie Davis in the Broadway revival of *Ain't Misbehavin'*, which garnered a Grammy nomination for Best Musical Show Album in 2009.

CARMEN RASMUSEN

✳ **HOMETOWN:** Bountiful, Utah

✳ **AUDITION SONG:** "Ribbon in the Sky" by Stevie Wonder

✳ **WORDS TO LIVE BY:** *"You've got a lot of power there. Wow."* —Olivia Newton-John

✳ **LIFE AFTER *IDOL*:** She was Simon's pet from the get-go and his personal choice for the wild card round, and after Carmen Rasmusen's sixth-place bow, she kept *Idol* close to her heart, appearing on the summer tour, subsequent all-star revues, and even additional TV stints, like when she teamed up with season four's Anthony Fedorov for the NBC show *Fear Factor*. Venturing out on her own, she released a 2007 country album, *Nothin' Like the Summer*, in conjunction with a book, *Staying in Tune*, in which the proud Mormon (who famously refused to wear revealing outfits during her *Idol* run) reflected on her values at home and experience in the entertainment business.

KIMBERLY CALDWELL

✳ **HOMETOWN:** Katy, Texas

✳ **AUDITION SONG:** "Superstition" by Stevie Wonder

✳ **WORDS TO LIVE BY:** *"I look at you, and I go, 'You know what? She's got mad vibes and mad personality.'"* Randy

✳ **LIFE AFTER *IDOL*:** Wasting no time transitioning from contestant to television host, fast-talking Texan Kimberly Caldwell landed a correspondent job at the FOX Sports Network within weeks of her seventh-place elimination. That led to a more permanent gig at the TV Guide Network, where Kimberly cohosted a variety of programs, including the popular *Idol Wrap* with Justin Guarini, and later P. Diddy's *Idol*-like show, *Starmaker*, and the Mark Burnett–helmed reality competition *Jingles*. But music remained an integral part of Kimberly's being and she continued to toil away at a singing career simultaneously. Seven years after she wowed the *Idol* judges, Kimberly landed a recording contract with Vanguard Records, releasing her debut single, the gritty "Mess of You," in 2010.

RICKEY SMITH

✳ **HOMETOWN:** Keene, Texas

✳ **AUDITION SONG:** "One Last Cry" by Brian McKnight

✳ **WORDS TO LIVE BY:** *"You were very good, man, I felt your personality, you sang well. I was impressed, dog. Very nice."* —Randy

✳ **LIFE AFTER *IDOL*:** Rickey Smith may have lost the *Idol* crown only four weeks into the top twelve, but his reputation for being Mr. Personality has remained a trademark of the fan favorite finalist. After entertaining audiences and fellow Idols alike on the season one summer tour and spending a couple years in Los Angeles, Rickey returned home to Texas and appeared in the stage show *Oz: The Musical* (written by future season nine contestant Todrick Hall) before finally settling down in Oklahoma City.

COREY CLARK

* **HOMETOWN:** San Bernardino, California

* **AUDITION SONG:** "Never Can Say Goodbye" by The Jackson 5

* **WORDS TO LIVE BY:** *"America, I promise, I won't forget the words this time, but I may surprise you."* —Corey Clark

* **LIFE AFTER *IDOL*:** He may have charmed the judges, but Corey Clark also broke the rules by not disclosing his prior arrest record. That led to a hasty dismissal from the competition followed by a headline-grabbing self-published book, a debut CD with disappointing sales, and then a string of additional legal problems.

JULIA DEMATO

* **HOMETOWN:** Brookfield, Connecticut

* **AUDITION SONG:** "Un-break My Heart" by Toni Braxton

* **WORDS TO LIVE BY:** *"You're one of the few people who've come in here and made it look effortless."* —Simon

* **LIFE AFTER *IDOL*:** Julia DeMato just made the season two summer tour by coming in tenth place, but upon returning home to Brookfield, Connecticut, after the forty-four-city run, continuing success in the entertainment world never quite materialized. She is still a local celebrity, hosting an annual *Idol*-like karaoke contest in nearby Norwalk. Occasional out-of-town bookings have allowed Julia the chance to reunite onstage with fellow finalists like Trenyce and Rickey Smith, and during season nine, she, along with *Idol* alums Ace Young, Diana DeGarmo, Jorge Núñez, and R. J. Helton, helped the nonprofit City Harvest feed New York City's hungry as part of Idol Gives Back.

CHARLES GRIGSBY

* **HOMETOWN:** Oberlin, Ohio

* **AUDITION SONG:** "Ribbon in the Sky" by Stevie Wonder

* **WORDS TO LIVE BY:** *"That's what entertainment is all about, you're definitely a crowd pleaser."* —Gladys Knight

* **LIFE AFTER *IDOL*:** Making the most of his short but sweet *Idol* ride, Charles Grigsby hit the ground running after his eleventh-place showing, releasing a self-titled EP in 2005, which included a cover of the soft rock staple "Baby, I Love Your Way," and letting his velvety-smooth voice speak for itself.

VANESSA OLIVAREZ

✳ **HOMETOWN:** Atlanta, Georgia

✳ **AUDITION SONG:** "Bohemian Rhapsody" by Queen

✳ **WORDS TO LIVE BY:** *"You do have a personality and in a real positive fun way, you have the acting ability of Bette Midler."* —Paula

✳ **LIFE AFTER *IDOL*:** Snappy comments to the judges may have cost Vanessa Olivarez the contest, but it didn't hamper the redhead from pursuing a career in music. After her twelfth-place elimination, the spunky Southern gal headed to Toronto, where she collaborated with songwriter James Collins on "The One," a ballad that reached number nine on the Canadian single charts, and also starred in the local production of *Hairspray*. Closer to her home turf, Vanessa had a writing credit on Sugarland's second album, *Enjoy the Ride*.

Greatest Hits

SUPERSTAR

RUBEN STUDDARD

FEBRUARY 11, 2003

Wearing the first of several 205 jerseys, season two's eventual winner earned instant front-runner cred with his soulful reinterpretation of The Carpenters' classic (also an R&B hit for Luther Vandross in 1983), which would later become Ruben's signature song and earn him a Grammy nomination (he lost to his idol Vandross). His top thirty-two performance in front of the judges had Randy on his feet and Paula asking for a hug. As for Simon, he had this to say: "Everything about that performance was sensational."

NEW YORK STATE OF MIND

KIMBERLEY LOCKE

APRIL 15, 2003

After weeks of Simon's insults—ragging on everything from her hair to her personality—Kimberley Locke started fighting back in a fierce way: She turned up the volume on her monster pipes (and toned down her runaway curls with a straightener) while also demonstrating the art of a nuanced performance, as she did with this Billy Joel classic, which prompted guest judge Smokey Robinson to comment, "As we say in the 'hood, you can saaang…"

UNCHAINED MELODY

CLAY AIKEN

MAY 13, 2003

With his transformation complete, the former-nerd-turned–bona-fide-*Idol*-contender brought down the house with the last of his top three performances. And the pressure was most certainly on: Not only was he closing out the episode that would decide who went to the finale, Clay was taking on one of the most iconic songs in American history, not to mention Simon's all-time favorite. And did he ever deliver! Wearing an understated black suit jacket and jeans, Clay delivered a pitch-perfect performance and took just enough liberty with the famous tune to make it unforgettable.

I'LL BE

JOSH GRACIN

FEBRUARY 25, 2003

America's first glimpse of Josh Gracin came by way of this top thirty-two performance, in which the future country star offered a taste of what was to come: strong vocals to match that brawny build. Josh's twang-tinged rendition of the Edwin McCain hit marched him straight to the top twelve, where he would demonstrate those hefty muscles by performing a set of push-ups on the *Idol* stage.

COME SEE ABOUT ME

TRENYCE

MARCH 11, 2003

She was Paula's pick after a powerful wild-card-round performance of Al Green's "Let's Stay Together," and to prove she belonged in the top twelve, Trenyce took on The Supremes during Motown Week, delivering a spot-on rendition of "Come See About Me" with songwriter Lamont Dozier seated at the judges' table. In the end, her ninety seconds onstage would make Simon eat his words. "Something I don't like doing, I have to congratulate Paula for championing you," he said. "That was outstanding."

COME TO MY WINDOW

KIMBERLY CALDWELL

FEBRUARY 4, 2003

Finalist Kimberly Caldwell was first to take the top thirty-two stage and looked to her own idol, Melissa Etheridge, for inspiration. "'Come to My Window' was me bringing out my sword," she says. "I remember Simon saying, 'That was brilliant!' I couldn't believe it. I was really proud and felt great about it. It's still the performance people come up and talk to me about."

Idol was still finding its sea legs on year two, but the frenzy was building and reached a fever pitch with the May 2003 finale. It was down to Clay Aiken and Ruben Studdard, two contestants from the South who'd barely hit a bum note all season long. One (Studdard) was a shoo-in from the start, the other more of a wild card. What were those final weeks like? We had season two's two Kims—Top three finalist Kimberley Locke and seventh placer Kimberly Caldwell—look back in pictures.

KL: When you get to the top three, it's intense, because you look back and see how many people didn't make it to that point. Then you look ahead and there's only a few people left. And you're like, "Oh my gosh, this is all coming to an end." I set goals for myself and my goal was to make it to the top three with Ruben and Clay. At that point, I didn't care who won because any of us deserved to win. But I think you have to find a happy place within yourself because it is nerve racking.

KL: We would be exhausted. On the show, we were always going, going, going, so when we'd sit down, my body felt like it was sleepy time. So we'd found our little spot to rest in the Coca-Cola room. We were talking and probably dozed off in the middle of the conversation.

KC: Even though we were go, go, go, there was still a lot of hurry up and wait. That's how we all became close—we'd be rushing and then have to wait for two hours, and then jump back up again and do a headstand...that was our bonding time—or sleeping time.

KL: You see yourself on those screens and think, "Oh gosh, that's what I look like across three million TV screens across the country." I remember the first time being on the *Idol* stage was so overwhelming. All those cameras are intimidating, you don't know how to work it at that point. You have to learn how to gain your audience at home through the camera.

KL: The group numbers were so cheesy, but fun at the same time. Ruben and Clay were always goofing off. People would step on cracks in the stage and almost fall down. This one was supposed to be very simple and all-American, but it felt more like a commercial.

KC: Yeah, but we all really enjoyed being onstage together and learning these things together. It's those moments when you look at each other and these friendships that you built and think how amazing it was to be there together.

KL: Randy is the coolest person. I had a lot of respect for him because he's done it all—he's an artist, musician, and a producer—so when he would give me advice, I'd listen to it.

KL: I love Nigel. He's smart, fun, witty, very creative and has a passion for music that came through on the show: from song selection to choreography and everything in between. I admire Nigel a lot—he's the walking vision for the show. He has gone out there, pounded the pavement, fought for himself—and look at him now.

KC: Nigel is amazing. He's always been like a guardian and caregiver to us. He really helped us through the processes and would be there for us. On the job he is very professional, but in between being an authority figure, he would crack a joke and then it was back to work.

KL: He can be very intense as well. One of my first memories of him was during Hollywood Week. We were auditioning in the hotel and he said, "Look to your right, look to your left. One of these people will not be here tomorrow." That moment stuck in my brain. It was very real and set the tone for the rest of the show.

KL: One thing we learned was to take time to rehearse whenever we could because there wasn't a lot of time. So I would take ten or fifteen minutes to practice singing on my own.

KL: That's Clay taking his moment. It's hard to find that quiet place to be by yourself, get in your own head, try to make sense of it all and focus. At the end of the day, it is a competition, and we were always thinking about what we were going to do next to win over the fans.

KC: I was an Oprah fanatic! I Tivo'd the show every day. She was backstage and I screamed. I wanted to go find her and I did not care how many security guards she had, I was going to meet Oprah! She shook my hand and put her other hand on top of my hand and I still do that to this day. I loved that. I told her, "This is like meeting God" and she laughed. She was very kind and sweet.

KL: She was intrigued by the show and wanted to know more about it, so she came to the set to interview us and it was just crazy. She brought her own production people and basically took over the place. It was pretty great to meet her and sit on the couch with her and have her be genuinely interested in us.

KL: The three of us were best friends. We bonded very early on in the show because we were in the same group on the very first group night—Ruben and I made it through and Clay didn't—so that was the first time we all prayed together. And our prayer was that Clay would come back in the wild-card round and we would all be in the top three.

KL: Chatting like two little girls, this is a great depiction of how close we were on the show. There are some true, real relationships that come out of *Idol*. Sometimes we get so caught up in the excitement of it all, and we forget about these moments. It's nice to see a picture that takes you back to such a special place.

KL: Being in the makeup chair, I took it as my time. Like, leave me alone. It's right before performance time so I'm getting my head in the game. It's like a locker room—time to focus on the night ahead, time for me to get my confidence up. There have been times when I've asked people to leave the hair-and-makeup room because if there's too much going on, it can be a distraction.

KC: Kimberley Locke came into the competition as a star and we saw her grow even more into one. When it comes to memorable Idols, if you say her name, people know exactly who you're talking about. She owns who she is and she is such a gorgeous girl.

KL: The night I got voted off, Paula was so sweet. I was sadder that the show was over than that I didn't win. It was such a great and truly unique experience; you really don't want it to end.

KC: I think what clinched it for Ruben was how lovable he was. He seems like this normal, down-to-earth guy, which he is. You can imagine yourself hanging out with him. And when you meet him, he's exactly like the person onstage with that smile and that warmth. Everybody could see themselves as a real friend of Ruben's.

KC: Clay was the guy next door—always funny, very outgoing and witty. Every single day, we saw him turn into more and more of a star—into who he is today.

KC: This was on finale night—the second red carpet we ever walked—we were all such goofballs. I hear from Rickey, Charlie, and Ruben all the time. They are such good-hearted people. None of those guys changed at all. They're still the exact same people as when they walked into auditions.

KL: During finale week, we each had to sing three or four songs so the quick changes in the back are seconds long. They would literally put up a makeshift changing area and there were two people there to help me get dressed. That's Dean Banowetz curling my hair.

KC: When Paula and Simon kissed during the finale, that was weird because we see them as brother and sister. They fight and bicker and joke, but they have unconditional love for each other.

KL: They kept it so on the down low. Nobody knew they were going to do that. I think they kept it that way on purpose so it became a side story. What are Paula and Simon gonna say to each other this week?

KL: When they announced the winner, I was sitting out in the middle of the audience, eight rows back on the aisle. I had placed my bet on Ruben winning because when I got voted off, my voters split their votes and Ruben had a lot of hype.

KC: It was fifty fifty for me. I thought Clay might have won, but the 205 shirts were taking over the audience. When they announced the results, we were ecstatic for Ruben because he was such a doll and such a talent.

CHAPTER 4: **RANDY JACKSON**

RANDY JACKSON 101

In the nine years that *American Idol* has been beamed into our living rooms, Randy Jackson has practically become a member of the family to tens of millions of viewers. Randy's laid-back attitude and frank but friendly observations positioned him as the perfect mediator between Simon's hard-as-nails approach and Paula's sweet critiques. Always ready to offer his trademark "Come on, dogg!" to a wayward contestant, or come to Paula's aid against Simon's tirades, Randy's knowledgeable but kind judging style quickly became the voice of reason in the competition.

And deservedly so; Randy logged more than twenty-five years in the music industry before joining *Idol,* so he knew a thing or two about working with artists. He began his career in the early eighties as a bassist for the enormously successful band Journey, then after A&R stints at several major labels, where he mastered the art of finding and nurturing talent, he went on to record albums with the likes of Mariah Carey, Tracy Chapman, and Celine Dion.

To that end, Randy's support of *Idol* contestants doesn't necessarily end when they're eliminated. He's been known to collaborate with several former finalists, including Kimberley Locke and Brooke White.

Away from the judges' table, Randy hosts a syndicated radio show and is the brains behind the MTV show *America's Best Dance Crew,* which brings together crews from across the country to compete for cash and bragging rights. As executive producer, Jackson implemented a format similar to *Idol*, with dancers counting on America's votes and a panel of judges to stay in the game. Going into its fifth season, the show is a smash hit that shows no signs of slowing down. You could say the same of Randy. An entrepreneur, a creative mind, a savvy business-man (Randy Jackson–branded glasses are hot sellers at Wal-Mart), and a music maker, Randy keeps his résumé always growing.

RANDY'S JOURNEY

AFTER BEING DIAGNOSED WITH TYPE 2 DIABETES, RANDY JACKSON GOT SERIOUS ABOUT SLIMMING DOWN, UNDERGOING GASTRIC BY-PASS SURGERY AND SHEDDING OVER 100 POUNDS.

2003 When TV viewers were first introduced to judge Randy Jackson, he tipped the scales at 350 pounds.

2004 It was during Season 3 that Randy decided to have the gastric bypass procedure, and the pounds slipped away quickly, as one can see in his suddenly oversized shirt.

2005 A year after the surgery, Randy was looking downright skinny as he made his entrance to the *Idol* studio.

2007 Many people struggle with their weight after surgery, so Randy wrote his book, *Body with Soul: Slash Sugar, Cut Cholesterol, and Get a Jump on your Best Health Ever*, to let his fans know of his personal struggle.

2008 Looking fit in a purple long sleeve and jeans, Randy was well on his way to his ultimate goal: lean and mean.

2010 While he's half the man he was in season 4—in girth only, 'natch—Randy's wardrobe had doubled, allowing him to experiment more, like with this Mr. Rogers sweater in his favorite colors.

FOUR (TO THE FLOOR) EYES

Randy's style has evolved over the years, from untucked dress shirts to fashion-forward designers, as has his flare of outrageous glasses, now considered one of the most successful brands for men's eyewear (really, the Randy Jackson Collection is number one at Wal-Mart). Take a brief look back at Randy's bespectacled life.

Randy's sky blue frames are perfect for a sunny red carpet day.

The purple frames may shield Randy from the harsh TV lights, but they won't save him from the off-key singing.

Randy takes his job seriously, and these wire-framed—I mean business—glasses aim to prove that. Randy's on-air vocabulary may be limited to "dude" and "dogg," but these smart-guy spectacles paint a different picture.

If there was any doubt about Randy's sense of style, this season eight pumpkin pair spoke volumes.

Blue is becoming to Randy. No wonder he opted for these special Finale Night frames—with handkerchief to match.

Randy might say these are some next-level frames, with open side slots that allow the eyes to breathe.

Making a bold statement with these plastic frames, Randy sports the brightest blue frames money can eye.

"DOGGMA" BY ANOOP "DOGG" DESAI

Whether you spell it "dog," "dawg," or "dogg," the familiar Randy Jackson-ism is as endearing to *Idol* fans as Ryan's "*This* is *American Idol!*" incantation or any of Simon's twisted metaphors. I dare anyone to do a Randy Jackson impression without using the word "dogg." It simply cannot be done. I furthermore dare anyone to use the word "dogg" seriously in a sentence without evoking some sort of said impression from one's audience. Is it possible that Jackson's signature phrase is this generation's "No whammy, no whammy, no whammy?" a phrase that won't make sense in twenty years, but will continue on as a benchmark of an era of American television? Maybe it's the new "Did I do thaaat?" or the new "I pity the fool." Maybe . . .

I'm not going to lie, it takes a while to get used to. Especially in person. Especially when it becomes your nickname . . . like, I don't know, Anoop Dogg. Sure, it was my fault. But after a lifetime of people mispronouncing and misspelling my name, you learn how to correct them in different ways. For a long time, I used the line "It's like Snoop with an A instead of an S." I'm sure there were others. So when Cowell infamously called me Anoopy before my first audition, it was second nature to spout off "No, it's Anoop. Like Randy, you could call

me Anoop Dogg." Yuk, yuk, yuks all around and then I actually started singing. I had no idea that it would evolve into a nickname people still yell at me as I walk down the street. It's also part of my name on Twitter, and generally has become something of an identifier. All thanks to Mr. Jackson's penchant for sobriquets.

Just when this word was disappearing from the American lexicon, going the way of "groovy," the Whig party, and the mighty buffalo, Randy Jackson brought it back. Thank goodness, too. Whenever "dude," or "bro," or "man," just won't suffice, there's now another option. Who let the dogs out? Randy Jackson, that's who. I'm not sure if he's cashed in on this, but I imagine a line of pet care products could be in his future if he wanted. But what does Randy actually mean by calling someone "dogg"? Dogs after all can be man's best friends or mangy curs. I'd like the think it's the former that lies at the heart of "dogg's" etymology. Then again, maybe Randy is a fan of hot dogs or a Georgia Bulldogs fan. Whatever the meaning or the origin, the truth is that the Big Dogg, Mr. Randy Jackson, will always be the true owner of the word in the eyes of *Idol* watchers. So cheers, Randy! Thanks for dogging *Idol* contestants to be the best they can be.

SEASON THREE BROUGHT THE TOUGHEST vocal
competition in the show's history, churned out two of *Idol*'s most
successful stars, and delivered what's undoubtedly one of the greatest TV moments ever: the crowning of winner Fantasia Barrino on
May 26, 2004.

Months earlier, Paula, Randy, and Simon realized they had their work
cut out for them as the females came out in full force, filling eight
of the top twelve spots and marked *Idol*'s first-ever all-girl final four.
Indeed, this diva-heavy lineup featured vocal chops unlike any the
show had ever seen. Fantasia's fierce, gospel-like performances
aside, season three also introduced the world to Jennifer Hudson,
who was famously eliminated in seventh place, but only after wowing the judges, the studio audience, and millions of TV viewers with
her extraordinary range and soulful delivery. And who could forget
wide-eyed youngsters like Diana DeGarmo, Leah LaBelle, and Jasmine Trias, who came to prove age had nothing to do with talent—
with two of those talented teens, Diana, then sixteen, and Jasmine,
seventeen, landing in the top four, alongside another impressive
R&B singer, LaToya London.

As for the guys, they scored points for originality. Red-haired John
Stevens was a sixteen-year-old Frank Sinatra throwback, Jon Peter
Lewis fully embraced his quirky cutie persona with Elton John–like
stylings, and sweet Southerner George Huff took his soulful sound
all the way to the top five. But in the end, it was Diana DeGarmo and
Fantasia who would face off in the finals, with DeGarmo coming in
second to Fantasia's flawless last performances with a record 65
million votes cast, more than the first two seasons combined.

Fantasia first told the judges she should be the next American Idol
because her voice was big, but her talent was bigger. Turns out she
was right, as she captivated audiences with her unique, raspy voice,
enthusiastic delivery, and natural stage presence. By the time she
sang her coronation song, "I Believe" (written by season two alum
Tamyra Gray), she'd made faithful believers of untold numbers—men,
women, and children alike—all inspired by her triumphant story.

CLASS *of*
04

SEASON 3 YEARBOOK

SEASON 3
WINNER!
2004

SEASON 3
RUNNER-UP
2004

AMY ADAMS

"Makeup Artist"

FANTASIA BARRINO

"Mom"

DIANA DEGARMO

"High School Student"

JENNIFER HUDSON

"Cruise Line Singer"

GEORGE HUFF

"Cook"

LEAH LABELLE

"High School Student"

"You are creating a battle of the divas." —Simon Cowell

"You can sing, man."
Randy Jackson

JON PETER LEWIS

"Student"

LATOYA LONDON

"Waitress-Bartender"

MATTHEW ROGERS

"Mortgage Banker"

JOHN STEVENS

"High School Student"

JASMINE TRIAS

"High School Student"

CAMILE VELASCO

"Waitress"

FANTASIA BARRINO

* **HOMETOWN:** High Point, North Carolina

* **AUDITION SONGS:** "Killing Me Softly" by Roberta Flack; "Rollin'" by Tina Turner

* **WORDS TO LIVE BY:** *"You're the best contestant we've ever had in any season."* —Simon

* **LIFE AFTER *IDOL*:** Season three's vivacious victor has upheld her reputation as "the best contestant ever," launching a successful career as a chart-topping artist, breakout Broadway star, best-selling author, and movie actress. In 2004, her coronation single, "I Believe," debuted at number one on the *Billboard* Hot 100 chart, and nabbed her three American Music Awards, becoming the best-selling single of the year. Her multiplatinum debut album, *Free Yourself*, entered the *Billboard* 200 at number eight, spawned two more hits, "Truth Is" and "Free Yourself," and earned Fantasia four Grammy nominations in 2006, the same year she released her follow-up, self-titled album. Her gold-certified sophomore album earned her three more Grammy nominations in 2008 and contained collaborations with heavy hitters Swizz Beatz, Missy Elliott, and Babyface.

Fantasia soon added "author" to her impressive résumé when she penned her *New York Times* best-selling autobiography, *Life Is Not a Fairy Tale.* The book focused on Fantasia's inspiring struggle with literacy, teen pregnancy, and faith, and was adapted into a Lifetime movie directed by Debbie Allen and starring Fantasia as herself. More than 19 million viewers tuned in to the movie's premiere, making it the second-most-watched movie in the network's twenty-two years.

Fantasia returned to the *Idol* stage in 2007, where she announced her upcoming role of Celie in Oprah Winfrey's Broadway adaptation of *The Color Purple.* Her performance garnered rave reviews and allowed Fantasia to flex her fiery vocals nightly to packed houses. The show reported a $34 million jump in sales since Fantasia's involvement, despite the fact that she missed half her scheduled performances due to

a tumor on her vocal cords. Following surgery, the resilient star rejoined the cast for stops in Los Angeles; Washington, D.C.; Chicago; and Atlanta. She'll take the role to the silver screen in Winfrey's film adaptation of the play. In 2010, she starred in the VH1 reality show *Fantasia for Real*, giving fans an inside look at the making of her third album, *Back to Me*. She performed the record's first single, "Even Angels" on *The Oprah Winfrey Show* and released its second single, "Bittersweet," in spring 2010, debuting it—where else—on the *American Idol* stage, which has become like her second home.

DIANA DEGARMO

✳ **HOMETOWN:** Snellville, Georgia

✳ **AUDITION SONG:** "Chain of Fools" by Aretha Franklin

✳ **WORDS TO LIVE BY:** *"You remind me of when Christina Aguilera was nice."* —Simon

✳ **LIFE AFTER *IDOL*:** Diana DeGarmo's sweet personality and enthusiastic performances

consistently wowed the crowd while week after week her powerful vocals and poise beyond her sixteen years impressed the judges. So much so that this talented teen made it all the way to the final two and went head-to-head against Fantasia in the finale, a huge feat in and of itself! After the *Idol* summer tour, Diana was signed to Nineteen Recordings/RCA Records and released her debut album, *Blue Skies* (featuring three tracks from future *Idol* judge Kara DioGuardi), in December 2004 with a cross-country promotional tour.

Diana then carried those pipes and charisma straight to New York City, where she would soon become a Broadway darling. Her stay on the Great White Way began with the role of Penny in *Hairspray*, which led to the lead role of Brooklyn in the 2006 national tour of *Brooklyn: The Musical* alongside one of her own personal idols, Melba Moore. Diana returned to Broadway's *Hairspray* for a second time in 2006, making her first appearance at New York's historic Carnegie Hall in 2007. In 2009, she joined the cast of *The Toxic Avenger*

as Sarah, and most recently starred as Sheila in the Broadway production of *Hair* opposite season five alum Ace Young. Next up for Diana: the starring role in the national tour of *9 to 5*.

JASMINE TRIAS

✳ **HOMETOWN:** Mililani, Hawaii

✳ **AUDITION SONG:** "I Will Always Love You" by Whitney Houston

✳ **WORDS TO LIVE BY:** *"Beautiful, just beautiful."* —Barry Manilow

✳ **LIFE AFTER *IDOL*:** You know you've made it when McDonald's names a meal after you! So it went for third-place finisher Jasmine Trias, whose "Jasmine Trio" meal was offered across the Philippines, where Jasmine's star continued to rise long after she took her final *Idol* bow. After heading home, the Hawaiian honey found she had millions of adoring fans across the globe waiting for her next move, so she took advantage of opportunities in markets near and far, starring in ads and using her influence to discourage youth from smoking, drinking, and other destructive behaviors.

In 2005, Jasmine released her self-titled debut album with Clockwork Entertainment and inked a deal with Universal Records for her international release. While it didn't make much of a splash in the U.S., the album was certified

platinum in the Philippines and prompted her to headline tours in Manila and Guam. The island beauty also found her place in television, acting as *TRL*'s season six *Idol* commentator and hosting her own TV show, *Pacific Groove,* in Hawaii. In 2009, Jasmine joined Hawaii's Society of Seven band at the Gold Coast Hotel in Las Vegas, where she wows crowds with nightly performances showcasing the silky-smooth style that made her a fan favorite from the start.

LATOYA LONDON

❋ **HOMETOWN:** Oakland, California

❋ **AUDITION SONG:** "Chain of Fools" by Aretha Franklin

❋ **WORDS TO LIVE BY:** *"You make me proud to be a songwriter."* —Barry Manilow

❋ **LIFE AFTER *IDOL*:** Fourth-place finisher LaToya London put up a valiant fight in season three with her impeccable control, extraordinary range, and rock-solid performances, which inspired Simon to declare her "the best singer in this competition," even in the company of powerhouses like Fantasia Barrino and Jennifer Hudson. After her Disco Week elimination, LaToya kept one foot firmly planted in the entertainment industry; she appeared in the national voting campaign Declare Yourself alongside Christina Aguilera, Andre 3000, and other music industry heavyweights, and later nabbed a guest cohosting gig on *Access Hollywood* before getting to work on her debut album. She signed with jazz label Peak Records in 2004 and released her first single, "Appreciate," featuring Roots front man Black Thought. The song peaked at number eight on the *Billboard* Singles chart and left fans across the country wanting for more. The following year, LaToya's debut album, *Love & Life,* came out to rave reviews, with *People* magazine calling it one of the best post-*Idol* albums to date and iTunes declaring it one of the best albums of the year. The jazzy, soulful, R&B record featured hits from legendary producer David Foster and spawned the single "State of My Heart,"

which landed at number forty on *Billboard*'s Adult Contemporary chart.

London's big voice led her to discover another calling: theater. In 2006 she made her stage debut playing the lead role in *Issues: We All Have 'Em*, alongside Angie Stone and Kim Fields. Later that year, she starred in the Los Angeles production of *Beehive* and received kudos for her performance. Some personal struggles followed for LaToya and by the end of 2006, she parted ways with her label and her husband. Not one to stay down or out for too long, LaToya fully embraced the challenging role of Nettie in the Chicago run of *The Color Purple,* alongside cast mate Fantasia Barrino and season six's LaKisha Jones.

GEORGE HUFF

❋ **HOMETOWN:** New Orleans, Lousiana

❋ **AUDITION SONG:** "You Are So Beautiful to Me" by Joe Cocker

❋ **WORDS TO LIVE BY:** *"I don't think you're aware of how good you really are."* —Simon

❋ **LIFE AFTER *IDOL*:** The lovable George Huff brought Southern charm and a deep, soulful sound to the *Idol* stage, ultimately going home

in fifth place as the last man standing, but wasting no time launching his postshow music career. George's debut album, *Miracles*, was released by well-known Christian label Word Records in October 2005, landing at number eight on the *Billboard* Gospel charts. That same year, Hurricane Katrina ravaged George's hometown of New Orleans and with his home destroyed, he was forced to relocate to Dallas and stay with family. Alluding to this trying time is the record's single, "Brighter Day," which was featured in the Tyler Perry film *Why Did I Get Married?* starring Janet Jackson. Not one to let tragedy shatter his dreams, Huff pressed on with his self-titled sophomore album, which was released in 2009 and featured the singles "Don't Let Go" and "Free."

JOHN STEVENS

* **HOMETOWN:** East Amherst, New York

* **AUDITION SONG:** "The Way You Look Tonight" by Frank Sinatra

* **WORDS TO LIVE BY:** *"You sounded very pure and innocent."* —Nick Ashford

* **LIFE AFTER *IDOL*:** John Stevens, the sixteen-year-old redhead from New York, stole the hearts of millions with his Rat Pack–inspired style and old-soul swagger. Affectionately

nicknamed Teen Martin, he eventually made it to sixth place on season three, racking up 4 million votes the night he was sent packing. Soon after, John signed with Maverick Records, releasing his 2005 debut, *Red,* featuring jazzy, big-band renditions of songs like The Beatles' "Here, There, and Everywhere" and Maroon 5's "This Love," as well as a duet with actress Erika Christensen. The album entered *Billboard*'s Jazz chart—an *Idol* first—in the number five spot. For his second studio effort, 2009's *Home for Christmas*, John crooned and cooed classic holiday tunes. Opting to continue his musical education, John attended the prestigious Berklee College of Music in Boston and graduated in 2009. He is currently performing with Boston's Beantown Swing Orchestra.

JENNIFER HUDSON

* **HOMETOWN:** Chicago, Illinois

* **AUDITION SONG:** "Share Your Love with Me" by Aretha Franklin

* **WORDS TO LIVE BY:** *"Hudson takes on Houston and wins!"* —Quentin Tarantino

* **LIFE AFTER *IDOL*:** In one of the show's most shocking eliminations ever—truly!—Jennifer Hudson, a girl with big hair and even bigger pipes was sent home in week seven, but it wouldn't be long before *Idol* fans saw her back in the spotlight.

In 2005, Jennifer landed the role of Effie in *Dreamgirls*, alongside heavy hitters Beyoncé Knowles, Jamie Foxx, and Eddie Murphy. It was her first go at the silver screen, and Jennifer did more than hold her own—she won an Oscar for Best Supporting Actress for her portrayal of the sassy, full-figured diva vying for a chance at the spotlight. Catapulted into superstardom, Jennifer collected Golden Globe and SAG trophies as well, graced the cover of *Vogue*, signed a record deal with Arista Records, and was cast in the first *Sex and the City* movie.

Her 2008 self-titled debut featured contributions from the likes of Ne-Yo, Missy Elliott, and Timbaland, and went on to sell more than

500,000 copies and earn Jennifer three Grammy nominations and one huge win for Best R&B Album. Its single, the aptly named "Spotlight," topped the charts and led to a nationwide tour with Robin Thicke. By then, the girl affectionately called J-Hud was on top of her game.

But among all the accolades that year came great tragedy with the loss of Jennifer's mother, brother, and nephew in the fall. Understandably, she retreated for a long period of mourning only to reemerge at Super Bowl XLIII in February 2009. Months later, she was performing for President Obama at the White House. Talk about a comeback.

More good fortune came her way as Jennifer and fiancé David Otunga welcomed their first child, son David Daniel Otunga, Jr., in August 2009. Since giving birth, she's shrunk from a size 16 to a size 6 and is flaunting her newly svelte bod as the national spokesperson for Weight Watchers. Five years after she said good-bye to *Idol*, Jennifer Hudson's star continues to rise, and only time will tell how high this alum will soar.

JON PETER LEWIS

❋ **HOMETOWN:** Rexburg, Idaho

❋ **AUDITION SONG:** "Crazy Love" by Van Morrison

❋ **WORDS TO LIVE BY:** *"You are the geekiest rock singer since Freddie and The Dreamers, but when you get into your geek mode, there's no one quite like you . . . Bravo!"* —Quentin Tarantino

❋ **LIFE AFTER *IDOL*:** His "Jailhouse Rock" performance during Movie Soundtracks Week was one of season three's most memorable moments, but it wasn't enough to save Jon Peter Lewis from elimination. Following his *Idol* exit, JPL, as he's called by friends (and Ryan Seacrest), released no fewer than three albums: a Christmas collection in 2005, his proper pop-rock debut, *Stories from Hollywood,* on his twenty-seventh birthday the following year, and in 2008, his sophomore effort, *Break the Silence,* which received rave reviews from critics.

After years of providing commentary as an *Idol* pundit for respected media outlets such as *Entertainment Weekly*, *Rolling Stone*, AOL Entertainment, and MTV, JPL parlayed that knowledge and created his own Internet TV show, *American Nobody,* which provides a sarcastic take on *Idol*, life in Hollywood, and pop culture. The *Los Angeles Times* called it "the most brilliant and biting satire of *American Idol* ever written."

CAMILE VELASCO

❋ **HOMETOWN:** Maui, Hawaii

❋ **AUDITION SONG:** "Ready or Not" by The Fugees

❋ **WORDS TO LIVE BY:** *"You're like a young Lauryn Hill."* —Randy

❋ **LIFE AFTER *IDOL*:** The Maui-born beauty, who wowed at the Honolulu auditions with her deep, smoky voice and exotic edge, made it only as far as week four, when her rendition of the Elton John hit "Goodbye Yellow Brick Road" fell short. But that didn't stop Camile Velasco from getting her own deal with Motown Records. In 2005, she released the single, "Hangin' On," and while the song failed to attract the critics' attention, it did resonate with the

Filipino American audience, leading to several gigs across the globe, including a performance with fellow Hawaiian heartbreaker Jasmine Trias in Maui. Camile and the label parted ways in 2006, never releasing a full-length album. Since then, she's appeared on subsequent seasons of *Idol* and, in 2007, Camile got to meet her real-life idol, Lauryn Hill, opening for her at Hawaii's Bob Marley Fest. Continuing to pursue music at her own pace, in 2008, Camile launched a weekly YouTube show, *CamileTV*, where she covers songs by her favorite artists.

AMY ADAMS

❋ **HOMETOWN:** Bakersfield, California

❋ **AUDITION SONG:** "Rescue Me" by Fontella Bass

❋ **WORDS TO LIVE BY:** *"You're phenomenal. I love your personality, and I love your stage presence."* —Paula

❋ **LIFE AFTER *IDOL*:** First, this magenta-haired California girl charmed the judges with her bubbly personality and ever-present smile. Then Amy Adams wowed the audience with her high-energy performances and exceptional voice control. Still, a Motown Week performance of "Dancing in the Street" sent her home in week three, having just made the cut for the fifty-two-city summer tour. Amy went on to helm the role of Narrator on the National tour of *Joseph and the Amazing Technicolor Dreamcoat.*

MATTHEW ROGERS

* **HOMETOWN:** Rancho Cucamonga, California

* **AUDITION SONG:** "Just Once" by James Ingram

* **WORDS TO LIVE BY:** *"I don't think I've ever met anyone who enjoyed being on television as much as you do."* —Simon

* **LIFE AFTER *IDOL*:** When Simon commented about Matthew Rogers's love of the camera, he didn't know he'd be predicting the contestant's next career move. The former football player with the big heart was ousted in week two, but not without leaving his mark on the competition. After his quick castoff, Matt used his *Idol* cred to break into television, fusing his love of broadcasting and sports as a correspondent for several shows, including *College Football on TBS*, *The Best Damn Sports Show Period*, *Access Hollywood*, and *Entertainment Tonight*. Hosting gigs followed, including stints on the Discovery Channel's *Really Big Things* and CBS's quirky reality show *There Goes the Neighborhood*. And, of course, there was the occasional return visit to *Idol*. On the home front, Matt married his longtime girlfriend in 2005 and the couple welcomed a baby boy, Brayden Douglas, in 2006.

LEAH LABELLE

* **HOMETOWN:** Seattle, Washington

* **AUDITION SONG:** *"I Believe in You and Me"* by Whitney Houston

* **WORDS TO LIVE BY:** *"You have this amazing, mature, Mary J. Blige–type of bluesy sound and you're very seasoned as a performer. All the little nuances and choreography you do onstage is perfect. It's subdued, but perfect and classy."* —Paula

* **LIFE AFTER *IDOL*:** The Bulgarian beauty surprised and impressed the judges with her soulful audition in New York City, but it would take more than a good voice to capture America's heart. Even after she was saved in the wild card round, the second chance kept Leah LaBelle on the show for only another week, as her performance of "You Keep Me Hangin' On" failed to live up to its title. The daughter of performer parents, she continued her musical pursuits at the esteemed Berklee College of Music in Boston with classmate and fellow finalist John Stevens.

SUMMERTIME

FANTASIA

MAY 25, 2004

It was season three's Cinderella moment: Fantasia, seated ever so slinkily on the *Idol* stage, delivered a sultry, pitch-perfect rendition of George Gershwin's "Summertime," which brought the judges to their feet and forever sealed her fate as one of *Idol*'s greatest talents. Simon noted, "There's something magical about what you just did." Indeed, it was a showstopper that led to a decisive victory and arguably the best performance in *Idol* history. Or so said Randy Jackson.

DON'T CRY OUT LOUD

DIANA DeGARMO

MAY 18, 2004

When Clive Davis chose Melissa Manchester's "Don't Cry Out Loud" as Diana DeGarmo's number for the top three, it was a chance for the young talent to soar. Her range as a vocalist was impressive and her pitch spot-on. As a performer, Diana proved that she could emote with believability and command the stage, two essential qualities to have as a future pop star. Paula called it "flawless" and Simon said, "Clive just booked your place in the final." Audiences agreed with the music mogul, who simply stated, "You did that song proud."

INSEPARABLE

JASMINE TRIAS

MARCH 16, 2004

Jasmine Trias's first top twelve performance, with her wearing what had become her trademark, a flower behind the ear, proved that beneath that soft-spoken, seemingly reserved demeanor was a vocal force to be reckoned with. Her spin on Natalie Cole's "Inseparable" had so much soul that it left the judges absolutely stunned. Paula called the performance her favorite of the night while Simon simply said, "Superb."

CIRCLE OF LIFE

APRIL 6, 2004

JENNIFER HUDSON

Jennifer Hudson's moving performance of Elton John's "Circle of Life" in week three was the spark that ignited the season's Battle of the Divas and set the stage for the fiercest female vocal competition the show had ever seen. A run-through for Sir Elton himself (that week's mentor) left the pop legend at a loss for words. "She blew me away [and] sent chills up my spine," he said. "That voice is amazing!" Show night turned out to be even more spectacular as J-Hud let that soulful voice rip, prompting Randy to call it her "best performance ever."

SOMEWHERE

APRIL 14, 2004

LATOYA LONDON

Movie Soundtrack Week featured a diverse selection of songs and styles, but when it came to bringing out the drama in a performance, LaToya London's near-perfect take on *Westside Story*'s classic "Somewhere" left the panel completely awestruck. Guest judge Quentin Tarantino summed it up best when he told the Bay Area beauty, "I got two words for you: Power. House."

JAILHOUSE ROCK

APRIL 15, 2004

JON PETER LEWIS

Every time Jon Peter Lewis got his Elvis on—three times in season three alone!—he busted moves nobody imagined he could have. So when his turn at the classic "Jailhouse Rock" drew the fewest number of votes during Movie Week, JPL let loose on elimination night as if he didn't have a care in the world. The high-energy performance brought the crowd to its feet and proved he had way more spunk than his "pen salesman" reputation suggested.

AMAZED

MARCH 24, 2004

MATTHEW ROGERS

Forget the teary farewell, it was all about laughs following Matthew Rogers's Country Week elimination. Opting for the anything-goes send-off, the husky jokester made a beeline for Simon Cowell while singing the Lonestar hit "Amazed." "Simon, when you touch me, I can feel how much you love me, and it just blows me away," he crooned, staring deep into the Brit's eyes as Paula grabbed on and clapped along. Simon was game, too, and even cracked the rare smile.

BATTLE ★ OF THE
DIVAS

FANTASIA BARRINO, JENNIFER HUDSON, and LATOYA LONDON: three power-house soul singers, but only one could be the American Idol. So played out season three's Battle of the Divas, launched by Jennifer's stirring rendition of Elton John's "Circle of Life" and ending with Fantasia's showstopping "Summertime" on Finale Night.

You could say Simon started this fight. He boldly named LaToya the best singer in the competition, then declared Fantasia the best *Idol* contestant ever. As for future Academy Award winner Ms. Hudson? Her huge voice and charismatic personality made her a standout from the start, but it would take the wild card round to give Jennifer a second chance at stardom.

With the top twelve in place, the divas went head-to-head, often leaving the judges speechless, but the voting didn't always reflect the panel's enthusiasm. In week six, the three received rave reviews for their Barry Manilow covers and were shocked to find themselves all in the bottom. Paula said Fantasia's straight-out-of-church rendi-

tion of Manilow's "It's a Miracle" was "a treat," while Simon added that she brought "excitement and danger" to the competition. LaToya also wowed the judges with her octave-defying version of "All the Time," which Paula called "incredible," while Jennifer's performance of "Weekend in New England" that night was both moving and fierce, and Barry Manilow himself declared that he "loved it." The next day, she went home.

So how did Jennifer get knocked out after only six performances, including a pitch-perfect rendition of Whitney Houston's "I Have Nothing?" It's one of the most debated eliminations in the history of *Idol* that essentially poses the question, who's the biggest diva of them all? In the end, they all won, as each went on to build thriving careers on the stage and screen. In fact, LaToya and Fantasia later reteamed on Broadway's *The Color Purple* while Jennifer stood strong as *Idol's* sole Oscar winner for her role in *Dreamgirls*, costarring a diva of the highest order (and the artist Jennifer listed as her biggest influence on an early *Idol* questionnaire), Beyoncé Knowles.

FANTASIA, SEASON THREE

American Idol's most touching and triumphant story has to be Fantasia Barrino. The nineteen-year-old single mom from High Point, North Carolina, arrived at the Atlanta auditions with a positive attitude, but her backstory was anything but. Assaulted in her teens, functionally illiterate, and barely able to support herself and her then-four-year-old daughter, Zion, she had only her angelic voice to lean on, and it carried her all the way to first place. Randy Jackson said on day one that the competition would be far less interesting without Fantasia—he neglected to say it would have been less inspiring, too.

ANTHONY FEDEROV, SEASON FOUR

Anthony Federov captured hearts across the country in season four with his soaring ballads and silky-smooth vocals—so very impressive, considering many thought that beautiful sound might never be heard at all. As a toddler in the Ukraine, Anthony underwent a tracheotomy to correct a birth defect in his windpipe. Doctors doubted he would ever speak again, and the scar (at the center of his throat) was visible when he defied the odds on the *Idol* stage. Anthony's baby face and powerful pipes took him all the way to the final four of the competition.

ELLIOTT YAMIN, SEASON FIVE

Health problems plagued Virginia's Elliott Yamin for much of his life, starting with eardrum replacement surgery at the age of thirteen, which left him with 90 percent hearing loss in his right ear. Three years later, he was diagnosed with type I diabetes, a condition that requires him to wear an insulin pump. Undeterred, Elliott honed his vocal chops by emulating soul greats like Stevie Wonder and Donny Hathaway, and joining a local jazz band. By the time he auditioned for *Idol* with "A Song for You," Elliott was ready and, with his ailing mom by his side, won America over in no time. Elliott made it all the way to third place, then released a successful debut album. Sadly, his beloved mother, Claudette, recipient of the season five Golden Idol for Proudest Family Moment Award, passed away in 2008.

DAVID COOK, SEASON SEVEN

David Cook's ascent to the *Idol* throne coincided with a much bigger battle: the fight for his brother Adam's life, symbolized with the initials AC adorning his guitar. Braving brain cancer, Adam was undergoing chemotherapy during all of season seven and, while very ill, managed to make the trip to Los Angeles to watch his brother in the top seven round. Though Adam did live to see his brother win *American Idol*, he succumbed to his disease in May 2009. David announced his brother's death the following day during the Race for Hope in Washington, D.C., where he completed the 5K race and raised $136,376 in Adam's memory. That fall, David performed "Permanent" in Adam's honor during the season eight finale. He later released the single on iTunes, donating all the proceeds to brain cancer research.

DANNY GOKEY, SEASON EIGHT

Only four weeks before he auditioned for *Idol*, Danny Gokey's beloved wife, Sophia, died during complications from surgery. The couple had been married for twelve years, and Sophia suffered from congenital heart disease from an early age. Although heartbroken, Danny explained that his wife was a huge fan of the show and had encouraged him to try out. The show highlighted Danny's struggle with grief throughout the season, causing some fans to wonder if he was trying to garner sympathy votes. He shrugged off such suggestions when he told MTV news, "I apologize to everybody if they feel like it's shoved down their face, but it's so fresh in my mind." Despite the critics, Danny used his wife's tragic death as inspiration and, in the process, encouraged others to live life to the fullest. Following his *Idol* run, Danny continues to devote his passion and energy to Sophie's Heart, a foundation he started in her name.

SCOTT MACINTYRE,

Diagnosed with Leber's congenital amaurosis at an early age, Scott had only a 2 percent field of vision when he tried out for *American Idol*, but that's never stopped him from chasing his dreams before, and this time was no different. Scott had credentials, too. Despite his impairment, he excelled at instruments and attended Canada's Royal Conservatory of Music, then Herberger College of the Arts at Arizona State University's prestigious Barrett Honors College. In 2005, he received another dangerous diagnosis—kidney disease. Scott spent ten months undergoing dialysis until he received a kidney transplant generously donated by his music professor's wife. The operation saved Scott's life, and the next year he hit the *Idol* stage.

American Idol

SEASON 3

BACKSTAGE PASS

CHAPTER 6: **PAULA ABDUL**

PAULA ABDUL 101

She was a Lakers girl, a choreographer, and a Grammy Award–winning recording artist when chosen to be one of three judges for a new show called *American Idol*. And while she may have been out of the spotlight for a while, it turned out Paula Abdul was a perfect fit. With a long résumé in entertainment (that began when she was discovered by the Jacksons during a basketball game), and no fewer than six hit songs, including the number one smash "Forever Your Girl," along with "Straight Up," "Cold Hearted," "Opposites Attract," and "Rush, Rush," Paula had the pop star credentials and stage experience, while being the choreographer for numerous tours (among them: Janet Jackson's *Control* trek) and films, including *Coming to America*, *Jerry Maguire*, and *American Beauty*, further demonstrated her show business savvy.

During her tenure on *Idol*, Paula was a constant cheerleader for the contestants, offering words of encouragement, complimenting their style, and getting up to dance whenever the mood struck her, while her famous verbal spats with Simon Cowell—and one headline-grabbing kiss—endeared her to millions. Week after week, year after year, people talked about what Paula wore and anticipated every word that came out of her mouth, whether or not it made any sense. In turn, she made pop culture history and for that, she'll forever be *Idol*'s girl.

PAULA'S PETS

EVERY TEACHER AND CLASSROOM IN AMERICA HAS A TEACHER'S PET–WHY SHOULD *AMERICAN IDOL* BE ANY DIFFERENT? PAULA, WHO ASSUMED THE ROLE OF CHEERLEADER AND SUPER-FAN FOR EVERY HOPEFUL TO TAKE THE STAGE, CERTAINLY HAD HER FAVORITES. HERE ARE BUT A FEW OF HER "PET" PERFORMERS.

JUSTIN GUARINI, SEASON ONE

During *Idol*'s first season, it was clear that Paula was Justin Guarini's biggest fan. Look no further than the week Paula feigned fainting, prompting Randy to yell, "Look what you did to Paula, man!" as Paula flopped on his shoulder. After Justin's signature song "Get Here" moved Paula to tears, she once again gushed, "Your quiet sincerity really made it masterful." And who can forget her reaction to his "Let's Stay Together"? "Two words: phe-nominal." Kelly Clarkson may have been crowned champ that season, but Justin will always be an Idol in Paula's eyes and heart.

TRENYCE, SEASON TWO

Back in season two, Clay Aiken was famously brought back as a wild card and went all the way to the finals, battling Ruben Studdard for the title. However, there was another pick that went almost as far, thanks to Paula. It was Trenyce's performance of "Let's Stay Together" that won Paula's heart. She commented, "Not only is she beautiful inside, she is beautiful outside. She is a star with one of the most amazing, polished voices. Her face lights up. Trenyce, my dear, I love you." Indeed, the two were tight. Trenyce later admitted that Paula even gave her the digits to her cell phone.

GEORGE HUFF, SEASON THREE

Season three was a topsy-turvy one in the Abdul universe. Initially, Paula chose seventeen-year-old Bulgarian songstress Leah LaBelle for the wild card pick after being impressed by her version of "Let's Stay Together" (what is it with Paula and that song?). But after Leah was dismissed the following week, Paula's heart was available for a new contestant and George Huff was the lucky recipient. Week after week, Paula commented on his sunny personality and ever-present smile. On Big Band Night, George grinned his way through the bubbly number "Cheek to Cheek" and Louis Armstrong's "What a Wonderful World." In true Paula fashion, she said George was "truly enchanting" and "charming as hell." When he was voted off in fifth place, Paula viewed America's decision as "sad."

ELLIOTT YAMIN, SEASON FIVE

Elliott Yamin already had America cheering for him after his moving rendition of Stevie Wonder's "If You Really Love Me," but it was Paula whom he constantly drove to tears and near emotional meltdowns. How much did Paula love Elliott? Let us count the superlatives: "brilliant," "phenomenal," "amazing," "fantastic." Elliott was her "funky white boy" and nothing could get in the way of that love fest. During Love Songs Week, after Elliott crooned Donny Hathaway's "A Song for You," Paula turned on the waterworks so hard that Simon couldn't help himself and burst out into laughter. Similarly, when Elliott finished third on season five, Paula was visibly upset, though she must have been incredibly proud when his first single, "Wait for You," became a top twenty hit one year later.

DANNY GOKEY, SEASON EIGHT

In a season that introduced the world to Bikini Girl and Adam Lambert, brought in Quentin Tarantino as a mentor, and featured the series' first ever legally blind contestant, Paula considered Danny Gokey's performances most unforgettable. Paula found herself "wowed," "slayed," and "grabbed" on a weekly basis. She loved his "brilliant" rendition of Carrie Underwood's "Jesus Take the Wheel" so much, she suggested even Underwood would buy a copy of it. And Paula repeatedly predicted Danny Gokey's march to the finals. Alas, it was Paula's top three pick of the Terence Trent D'Arby song "Dance Little Sister" that ended Danny's journey, and she was visibly fighting back tears as his tribute video played. She was right about one thing, though: Danny had a knack for country music, and is now recording and performing it for a living.

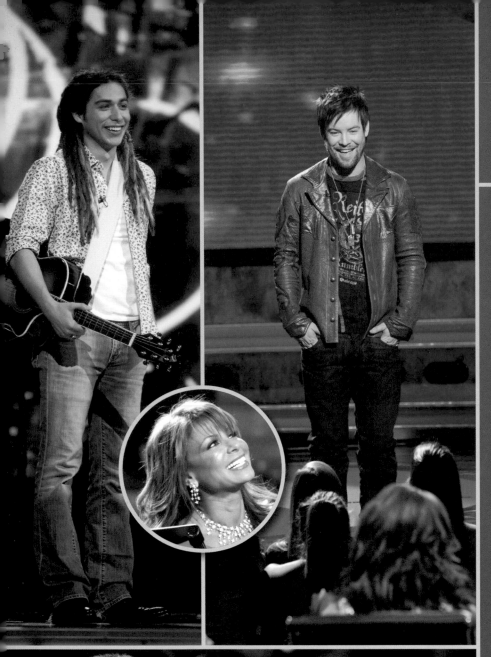

ABDULISMS

One of the most endearing aspects to Paula's personality is her sometimes-nonsensical musings that reference everything from animals to colors and food. Oh, Paula . . .

WHEN THE MATH DOESN'T QUITE ADD UP . . .

"I'm not trying to stutter twenty times but what if I said I'm one of your biggest fans?" —to Chris Daughtry after he performed Creed's "What If" for Songs of the 2000s Week

CURIOUS COMPARISON . . .

"I don't know whether we should give you a record deal or a straitjacket!" —to Taylor Hicks following his rendition of "Crazy Little Thing Called Love"—complete with his staple moves—during season five's Queen Week

COLORFUL COMMENTARY . . .

"You are a blend of every favorite color that I know." —to Jason Castro after his first proper top twenty-four performance, The Lovin' Spoonful's "Daydream"

TOO MUCH DESCRIPTION!

"David, you are ridiculous. I wanna just squish you, squeeze your head off, and dangle you from my rearview mirror." —to David Archuleta following his moving first rendition of John Lennon's "Imagine"

COMPLIMENT OR INSULT? THE JURY'S STILL OUT . . .

"You are like a dependable dog." —to Carly Smithson, who chose Cyndi Lauper's "I Drove All Night" as her 1980s Week song

ANIMAL INSTINCTS . . .

"The high notes that you hit, I think my Chihuahuas are gonna come join you onstage." —reacting to Michael Johns's "We Will Rock You"/"We are the Champions" Queen medley

7

CHAPTER 7: **SEASON FOUR**

A COUNTRY MUSIC SUPERSTAR was born in the summer of 2004. That's when farm girl Carrie Underwood arrived, from Checotah, Oklahoma, to St. Louis, Missouri, where *American Idol* auditions were taking place. She was one in a sea of 100,000, but there was something special about her—all three judges could see that instantly—and nine months later, she emerged victorious, the people's choice and a shining example of the *Idol* dream realized.

By year four, the show had truly found its footing, but not without making a few tweaks. The age limit was raised to twenty-eight, opening the door to season four's two longhairs, runner-up Bo Bice and sixth-placer Constantine Maroulis, both of whom just made the cutoff. The audition rounds (seven cities in total) also featured a handful of guest judges, including Brandy, LL Cool J, and Gene Simmons of Kiss. And after season three's female-heavy lineup, the semifinals ensured an even playing field for both genders as twelve guys and twelve girls competed separately for the twelve available spots.

But perhaps the biggest change in the show was also its greatest accomplishment: credibility—what drove not just the winner and much-touted rockers Bo and Constantine to try out, but the likes of Anwar Robinson, a teacher from New Jersey; Anthony Federov, a Ukranian-born hopeful who overcame a tracheotomy in his bid to become a singer; and female powerhouses Nadia Turner and Vonzell Solomon, who, like Fantasia before them, stirred the souls of studio audience members and TV viewers alike.

More than 500 million votes were cast that year, culminating in an all-star finale that would set the bar for all future season closers and start a tradition that continues until today: duets. Indeed, long before she opened for Rascal Flatts, Carrie got to perform with them on the Kodak Theatre stage. As for Bo, he was able to cross one giant achievement off his to-do list: sing "Sweet Home Alabama," not in a cover band, but with the members of Lynyrd Skynyrd! Kenny G and Babyface also made appearances as part of group numbers and medleys fine-tuned after months of intense competition.

So out of all that talent, what clinched it for Carrie? Near-flawless execution the whole way through, but especially on songs like Martina McBride's "Independence Day," which she belted with patriotic passion on 1990s Week and chose to reprise for the finale. Bo, for his part, was a formidable opponent, embracing his inner rock star on The Black Crowes' "Remedy" and Skynyrd's "Freebird." But in the end, it was Simon who would utter "I told you so" for correctly predicting that Carrie would not only win but also outsell every Idol in the show's history.

CLASS *of* 05

SEASON 4 YEARBOOK

"You are a gift to the sixty million people who watch this show." —Paula Abdul

SEASON 4
RUNNER-UP
2005

BO BICE

"Guitar Store Clerk"

LINDSEY CARDINALE

"College Student"

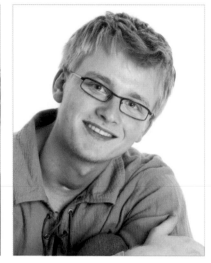

ANTHONY FEDOROV

"Student"

MIKALAH GORDON

"High School Student"

CONSTANTINE MAROULIS

"Musician"

ANWAR ROBINSON

"Music Teacher"

"The second you smile, it melts America's heart." —Paula Abdul

SCOTT SAVOL

"Corrections Officer"

JESSICA SIERRA

"Nanny"

NIKKO SMITH

"Singer"

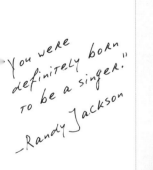

"You were definitely born to be a singer."
—Randy Jackson

VONZELL SOLOMON

"Mail Carrier"

NADIA TURNER

"Bartender-Waitress"

CARRIE UNDERWOOD

"College Student"

SEASON 4
WINNER!
2005

"You are the antidote to karaoke hell."
—Simon Cowell

"Country pop is your element, it just radiates from you, not only in your voice, but in your face and your body. You really nailed it, congratulations."
—Clive Davis

Looking back with the season five champ

What was it like the first time you were in front of the judges?

Carrie Underwood: I walked in to sing to them and was so amazingly nervous, but they got right down to business. I was singing, and Simon stopped me. I thought it was a bad thing. I figured he wouldn't do that if he thought I was doing a good job. But they sent me through!

You never found yourself in the bottom three, but did you dread possibly ending up there?

CU: I figured that it was only a matter of time, really. I still have no idea how I managed to escape the bottom three! Even when you feel like you have an awesome performance, that really means nothing. Anyone can end up in the bottom at any point! No one is safe!

How did you feel about Simon's comment that you would be the most successful *Idol* contestant ever?

CU: At the time, I was really worried that it would make the other contestants not like me, plus I was worried that people would purposely not vote for me to "show him." Even now, I still feel like it was an ambitious comment to make. It was flattering and made me worry at the same time!

Who was your favorite judge?

CU: I was always a fan of Randy. And when I was on the show, he was a favorite as well. He would deliver constructive criticism and that's what we contestants needed—someone to tell us how to get better. And since I've been on the show, he remains a favorite. Randy's always there to help me when I need some advice about musicians. He knows *everybody!*

The show looks so polished on screen, but what's it like behind the scenes?

CU: It looks much smaller in person. Backstage was always a mess of cables and lighting rigs. People were always running around, but in the end, it always looked amazing!

What were your first thoughts after hearing you won?

CU: I had no thoughts, only feelings. I felt so excited and elated! I remember seeing my mom in the audience and thinking, "I have to hug her." So I pulled her onstage with me. I love those pictures of us hugging. I also remember being afraid of the pyro that was going off behind me. I knew there was a lot of product in my hair that night, and I was scared a stray spark would catch my locks on fire!

You've returned to perform on the show no less than ten times. Why is it important to you to keep coming back to *Idol?*

CU: I owe everything to *American Idol.* I am a part of that family. Just because you move away from home doesn't mean that you stop being a part of your family! I love *American Idol* and love seeing the new batches of contestants that come through it. I am so blessed and hope that I always have a place on that show!

CARRIE UNDERWOOD

* **HOMETOWN:** Checotah, Oklahoma

* **AUDITION SONG:** "I Can't Make You Love Me" by Bonnie Raitt

* **WORDS TO LIVE BY:** *"You're not just the girl to beat, you're the person to beat. I will make a prediction: not only will you win this show, you will sell more records than any other previous* Idol *winner."* —Simon

* **LIFE AFTER *IDOL*:** If ever there were a model American Idol, season four victor Carrie Underwood would easily win that title. It's hard to believe this former "farm girl," a captivating performer and stunning beauty with an otherworldly voice, went undiscovered for years. But it comes as no surprise that Carrie best-selling Idol of all time.

Her meteoric rise to the top of the charts began not long after singing her final notes on *Idol*. Carrie's coronation song, "Inside Your Heaven," landed at number one in June 2005, plus her debut album, *Some Hearts*, was also a smash right out of the gate, selling 315,000 copies in its first week of release. Five years later, that number would balloon to 7 million, proving Simon Cowell's prediction right (see "Simon's Always Right," page 28), but first the crossover hits "Jesus Take the Wheel" and "Before He Cheats," the latter of which spent more than a year on the Billboard Hot 100.

As Carrie was racking up album sales, becoming a radio staple, and logging thousands of miles on the road touring as a headlining act, the nominations started pouring in. The Academy of Country Music Awards, Country Music Association Awards, American Music Awards, and Country Music Television Awards, just to name a few, eventually led to a Grammy win for Best Female Country Vocal Performance and Best New Artist in 2007.

The accolades only mushroomed from there. In 2008, Carrie was inducted as a member of the Grand Ole Opry, and a year later, she was named Entertainer of the Year by the Country Music Association. Meanwhile, Carrie released two more multiplatinum albums, 2007's *Carnival Ride* and

2009's *Play On*, and made dozens of television appearances, including ten return visits to *Idol* alone. She also hosted her own FOX Christmas special in 2009, followed by several concert specials for CMT.

Carrie, who married ice hockey player Mike Fisher in July 2010, uses the rest of her time to lend support to various charitable causes, from cancer research to music in schools, but animals are undoubtedly closest to this country girl's heart, which just goes to show, you can take the girl out of the farm, but you can't take the farm out of the girl . . .

BO BICE

* **HOMETOWN:** Helena, Alabama

* **AUDITION SONG:** "Whipping Post" by The Allman Brothers Band

* **WORDS TO LIVE BY:** *"You know exactly who you are, I know exactly the kind of record that you should make, and let me tell you that's a very hard thing, that's why I think a lot of people haven't made it, you are definitely on your way."* —Randy

* **LIFE AFTER *IDOL*:** A second-place finish awarded Bo Bice his own recording contract with RCA Records, and on June 21, 2005, the Southern rocker released his debut single, "Inside Your Heaven," knocking Carrie Underwood's version of the same song out of the

number one spot—a *Billboard* first! A month later, Bo was onstage with Phish front man Trey Anastasio at the Bonnaroo Music Festival in front of more than 75,000 people. That appearance led to walk-ons with Willie Nelson and a guest spot on a Carlos Santana record, all in advance of his first album, *The Real Thing*, which came out in December 2005 and featured the Kara DioGuardi–penned title track, a radio staple even today.

While the album performed well and was certified gold, Bo was plagued with health problems for much of 2006 (suffering from an intestinal condition that resulted from a previous surgery), but came back stronger in 2007 when he released his sophomore effort, *See the Light*.

Of course, there's no denying Bo's star power, which he often uses to promote worthy causes. He's traveled to Afghanistan and Kuwait to perform for the troops on several occasions.

At home in Nashville, where he's built a top-of-the-line studio, Bo is a husband and father of three, all sons.

VONZELL SOLOMON

* **HOMETOWN:** Fort Myers, Florida

* **AUDITION SONG:** "Chain of Fools" by Aretha Franklin

* **WORDS TO LIVE BY:** *"You have this innate ability to connect with an audience and tap into their heartstrings . . . this magic happens, which is just bone-chilling and beautiful."* —Paula

LIFE AFTER *IDOL*: Finishing third after Bo and Carrie put Vonzell Solomon in good vocal company, but a record deal never materialized for the Florida powerhouse. Undeterred, she formed her own independent label, Melodic Records, and released the album *My Struggle* in 2007, adding "Baby V" to her name. After so many weeks on the *Idol* stage, Vonzell's comfort zone was clearly fine in front of a live audience, as she went on to costar in theater productions with fellow season four alums Mikalah Gordon and Scott Savol. And the show continues to permeate Vonzell's daily life, at least during the season when she provides *Idol* commentary on her own YouTube channel.

ANTHONY FEDOROV

❊ **HOMETOWN:** Trevose, Pennsylvania

❊ **AUDITION SONG:** "Angel" by Jon Secada

❊ **WORDS TO LIVE BY:** *"I think you did a fantastic job and I think the producers got it absolutely right."* —Simon

❊ **LIFE AFTER *IDOL*:** Anthony Fedorov's affinity for ballads—and constant comparisons to Clay Aiken—earned him enough fan votes to come in at fourth place, and that following stuck with the Ukraine-born crooner, who underwent a tracheotomy as a child (and defied the odds by becoming a singer), long after the com-

petition ended. In his post-*Idol* life, Anthony landed leading roles in a variety of theatrical productions, including off-Broadway's *The Fantasticks* and *Joseph and the Amazing Technicolor Dreamcoat* for which he received rave reviews. Other noteworthy appearances include Anthony's 2009 performance at the BMI Latin Awards in honor of Gloria Estefan and his stroll down the red carpet at the 2006 CMA Awards with his good pal Carrie Underwood.

SCOTT SAVOL

❊ **HOMETOWN:** Shaker Heights, Ohio

❊ **AUDITION SONG:** "Superstar" by Luther Vandross

❊ **WORDS TO LIVE BY:** *"You've had more escapes than Houdini."* —Simon

❊ **LIFE AFTER *IDOL*:** Dubbed "Scotty the Body" by Ryan Seacrest, Scott Savol had a deep voice that matched while his song choices brought out a sensitive side. Riding the underdog wave through many rounds of the competition, Scott made a more than impressive showing when he exited in fifth place. In his

post-*Idol* life, Scott joined fellow season four alum Vonzell Solomon along with season one's R. J. Helton, season two's Carmen Rasmusen, and season six's Haley Scarnato and Brandon Rogers in the Branson, Missouri, all-star revue *America's Favorite Finalists*. Offstage, he married girlfriend Rochelle Waddell in June 2006 and has a son, Brandon, born in 2010.

CONSTANTINE MAROULIS

❊ **HOMETOWN:** New York, New York

❊ **AUDITION SONG:** "Cryin'" by Aerosmith

❊ **WORDS TO LIVE BY:** *"You're a perfect role model for guys to get into musicals. You're the coolest of cool."* —Paula

❊ **LIFE AFTER *IDOL*:** Charisma and natural showmanship made Constantine Maroulis a standout early on in the competition, and the show business world immediately took notice. Soon after his sixth-place finish, the brooding rocker scored a development deal with Kelsey Grammer's production company, Grammnet.

Furthering his TV career, he landed a recurring role on the CBS soap opera *The Bold and the Beautiful*, playing a singer and record producer. That same year he also released his debut album, simply titled *Constantine*. But in returning to his native New York City, Constantine found his true calling on Broadway. He joined the cast of *The Wedding Singer* in 2006, then the quirky musical *Jacques Brel Is Alive and Well and Living in Paris*, but it was his starring role in the Broadway sensation *Rock of Ages*, which would garner Constantine nearly as much recognition as his ten-week *Idol* run, not to mention a Tony Award nomination for Best Performance by a Leading Actor in a Musical. Indeed, more than five years after performing "Nights on Broadway" for *Idol's* 1970s dance Music Week, he's living it.

NADIA TURNER

* **HOMETOWN:** Miami, Florida

* **AUDITION SONG:** "Until You Come Back to Me" by Aretha Franklin

* **WORDS TO LIVE BY:** *"In a competition full of hamburgers, you are a steak."* —Simon

* **LIFE AFTER *IDOL*:** As a former Dolphins cheerleader and a veteran of child pageants, Miami-bred Nadia Turner was accustomed to putting on a show, which is exactly what she did week in and week out on *Idol*—if not with her fierce vocals, then another high-volume trait: her hair. After making it to eighth place, Nadia returned to her native South Florida and continued to pursue music while also taking up acting. She landed a role in the urban romantic comedy *Lord Help Us* in May 2007 and released her debut single, the gritty rocker "Standing on Love," in 2008.

ANWAR ROBINSON

* **HOMETOWN:** Elizabeth, New Jersey

* **AUDITION SONG:** Unconfirmed

* **WORDS TO LIVE BY:** *"Your voice is truly your instrument and it's an entire orchestra, and the way you take risks on songs that we've heard so many renditions of, you breathe new life into these songs. Beautiful."* —Paula

* **LIFE AFTER *IDOL*:** The judges loved him, but Anwar Robinson, the perpetually smiling music teacher from New Jersey, made it only as far as ninth place. Dance music from the 1970s signaled the end of his *Idol* run, but it wouldn't be his last time entertaining a captive audience of several hundred. Anwar spent much of 2007 and 2008 as a cast member in the international tour of *Rent*. Upon his return, he released his first single, the sultry R&B track "Night's Hot," followed by the celebratory "Exceptional" in September 2009. Outside of music, Anwar participates in a number of charities, including those devoted to breast cancer awareness and promoting performing arts in schools.

NIKKO SMITH

* **HOMETOWN:** St. Louis, Missouri

* **AUDITION SONG:** "All I Do" by Stevie Wonder

* **WORDS TO LIVE BY:** *"I just wanna bring it back to real music and real singing and make the people not just in America but all over the world feel good about music."* —Nikko Smith

* **LIFE AFTER *IDOL*:** He was eliminated in the semifinals, then brought back when Mario Vasquez abruptly left the competition for "personal reasons." No wonder they called

Nikko Smith "the Comeback Kid." Granted, he was the first of the top twelve guys to go, but not before making a strong impression with his Usher-like style and vocals. Upon returning home to St. Louis, Nikko continued to perform locally and released his debut album, *Revolution*, in 2008.

JESSICA SIERRA

❋ **HOMETOWN:** Tampa, Florida

❋ **AUDITION SONG:** "At Last" by Etta James

❋ **WORDS TO LIVE BY:** *"I like your voice, I like the kind of husky tone you have."* —Randy

❋ **LIFE AFTER *IDOL*:** Making the most of her top ten spot, the smoky-voiced Jessica Sierra hit the ground running following her elimination, performing for the troops in Iraq and Afghanistan in 2006 and appearing at numerous corporate events. But a year later, Jessica was plagued by legal troubles. Realizing that she needed treatment for her addictions, Jessica checked into *Celebrity Rehab with Dr. Drew,* where she underwent intensive therapy, later

televised as part of the VH1 reality show. With her recovery came musical inspiration in the form of her debut EP, *Deepest Secrets*, which included the single "Unbroken," both released in 2007. Now sober for more than three years, Jessica has added "mom" to her résumé, giving birth to son, Kayden, in 2009.

MIKALAH GORDON

❋ **HOMETOWN:** Las Vegas, Nevada

❋ **AUDITION SONG:** "Lullaby of Birdland" by Ella Fitzgerald

❋ **WORDS TO LIVE BY:** *"Personality, personality, personality, you've got that going on!"* —Randy

❋ **LIFE AFTER *IDOL*:** The sassy former cheerleader was compared to comedienne Fran Drescher so often that it only made sense to pair the two on-screen, and so Mikalah Gordon landed a role on the WB show *Living with Fran* mere months after her eleventh-place *Idol* finish—playing a Broadway singer, 'natch. Other television appearances followed, including a guest-starring stint on *The Unit*, a field correspondent gig on *The Tyra Banks Show,* and even a return to the singing competition circuit, in the form of the CMT show *Gone Country 2*. Never one to leave her *Idol* family far behind, Mikalah also took a cue from the Ryan Seacrest handbook and tried her hand at guest hosting the season seven and eight finales for FOX.

LINDSEY CARDINALE

❋ **HOMETOWN:** Ponchatoula, Louisiana

❋ **AUDITION SONG:** "Standing Right Next to Me" by Karla Bonoff

❋ **WORDS TO LIVE BY:** *"You have a very interesting voice, it's very unique, it's hypnotic to me and very pure."* —Paula

❋ **LIFE AFTER *IDOL*:** After surviving the semifinals, Lindsey Cardinale got to experience only one week on *Idol*'s big stage before being voted off. She returned home to Louisiana as a local celebrity, but learned soon enough that

fame has its pros and cons. A few years later, Lindsey decided to go back to college, attending Nashville's Belmont University to study journalism with a minor in songwriting. While on the performing front, she joined *Idol* alums Nikki McKibbin, Trenyce, Nikko Smith, and others for *American Christmas,* a holiday musical revue featuring an assortment of former contestants.

INDEPENDENCE DAY

CARRIE UNDERWOOD

MARCH 29, 2005

Carrie turned in solid performances throughout the competition, including her powerhouse rendition of Heart's "Alone" and a heart-stopping cover of Air Supply's "Making Love Out of Nothing at All," the final note of which prompted Randy to exclaim, "You can blow, dude!" But it was Underwood's shining moment when she took the stage and belted Martina McBride's "Independence Day." This was the week she showed her country colors, a preview of what the future Golden Girl had to offer. Randy couldn't use the word "great" enough. Simon told Carrie she had the "It" factor, which turned out to be a dead-on analysis. No wonder Carrie would encore the performance for her final two pick.

IN A DREAM

BO BICE

MAY 17, 2005

One of the most talked about performances of season four was Bo Bice's a cappella performance of "In a Dream." Bice first auditioned with this song, but the judges asked him to sing something more familiar before handing him the golden ticket. Still, he chose to perform the song again in front of Clive Davis, who told him he was getting "stronger every week." Randy loved that Bo brought the show back to its audition roots, and said, "You are as good now as you were then." Paula told him he was a "gift." Simon joked that Bice may have "just put thirty-four musicians out of work." The performance was so strong, many tried to duplicate it in subsequent auditions, but none has held up to the original.

BOHEMIAN RHAPSODY

CONSTANTINE MAROULIS

APRIL 12, 2005

Undoubtedly season four's resident heartthrob (Simon called him "smoldering Idol"), Constantine brought his sex appeal and flair for the theatrical together in one simmering pot when he chose Queen's "Bohemian Rhapsody" during The Year You Were Born Week. The screaming girls were so loud during parts of the song, it was as if the whole audience had been waiting just for this performance. Paula declared him "the one to beat" while Simon would characterize it only as "astonishing," unclear as to whether he meant it in a positive way. Still, Constantine knew his fan base, to which this standout performance appealed directly.

BEST OF MY LOVE

VONZELL SOLOMON

MARCH 22, 2005

Vonzell Solomon went all the way to number three in season three, and the week America stood up and took notice of the former postal worker's vocal chops was when she chose to cover The Emotions' "Best of My Love." Vonzell's performance had it all: vocal runs, perfect control, and a display of undeniable stage presence. Paula told Vonzell that her personality and vocals came out with the risky performance, and Simon manage to squeeze out a compliment: "Since the first time you have been in this competition, people are going to remember you," he said. Truer words were never spoken.

YOU DON'T HAVE TO SAY YOU LOVE ME

NADIA TURNER

MARCH 15, 2005

A rich, velvety tone took Nadia Turner's showstopping rendition of Dusty Springfield's "You Don't Have to Say You Love Me" to another level, prompting Simon to utter one of his more famous lines, "In a competition full of hamburgers, you are a steak." Not to be outdone, the following week, Nadia debuted the show's first ever fauxhawk, which would ignite water cooler chatter from coast to coast a good two years ahead of Sanjaya!

Carrie Underwood

HOME SWEET HOME:

WITH MORE RETURN VISITS THAN ANY OTHER WINNER BEFORE OR AFTER, YOU COULD CALL THE *IDOL* STAGE CARRIE UNDERWOOD'S HOME SWEET SECOND HOME.

Season Five • **"Jesus, Take the Wheel"** • March 2, 2006

Carrie's first trip back to the *Idol* studio was an unforgettable one as she premiered her debut single, "Jesus, Take the Wheel"—a song that has made almost as many appearances on the show as the season four winner.

Season Five • **"I Made It Through the Rain"** • May 24, 2006

Joining Katharine McPhee and Taylor Hicks, the last two contestants standing, for the season five finale, Carrie delivered one-third of the crowd-pleasing ballad, "I Made It Through the Rain."

Season Six • **"Wasted"** • March 8, 2007

Season six's top sixteen got an early taste of stardom when Carrie came by to perform her number one country hit "Wasted."

Season Six • **"I'll Stand by You"** • May 23, 2007

Carrie's season six finale number was her moving cover of The Pretenders' "I'll Stand by You," an encore performance from a month earlier when she sang the same song with Kelly Clarkson and Rascal Flatts.

Season Seven • **"Last Name"** • May 21, 2008

For the season seven finale, a svelte Carrie took the Nokia Theatre stage for a rousing rendition of "Last Name," off her second album, *Carnival Ride*.

Season Eight • **"Home Sweet Home"** • May 19, 2009

Bookending the final two performances on season eight was Carrie's cover of the Mötley Crüe ballad "Home Sweet Home," which also served as the elimination song for that year.

Season Nine • **"Undo It"** • May 26, 2010

Ready to rock in skintight leather pants and a to-die-for half vest, Carrie performed "Undo It" from her third album, *Play On*, during the season nine finale. The song was written by Carrie with Kara DioGuardi.

OUR NEXT
CONTESTANT
IS OUT OF
ALABAMA.

American Idol

SEASON 4

BACKSTAGE PASS

CHAPTER 8: **FAN FRENZY**

SIMON COWELL ALWAYS SAID THAT *AMERICAN IDOL* BEGINS AS A COMEDY AND ENDS AS A DRAMA. INDEED, NOTHING BRINGS OUT THE WACKY QUITE LIKE THE FIRST WAVE OF AUDITIONS. HERE ARE SOME OF THE SHOW'S MOST MEMORABLE CHARACTERS.

RENALDO LUPAZ

Among the most memorable auditions ever was Renaldo Lupaz from Nevada, who decided to go for *Idol* with an original song. Clad in a white birdlike ensemble, with Simon's named etched on his hat, he was, as Ryan noted, "ready to take flight." The song "We're Brothers Forever" was catchy and by the end of his audition, all three judges were singing along, Paula and Randy were waltzing, and Simon was charmed, predicting a hit record. The song later became a ringtone, and Renaldo returned twice in subsequent finales.

WILLIAM HUNG

The king of wacky auditions, William Hung became a national phenomenon following his famed rendition of Ricky Martin's "She Bangs" complete with jerky dance moves. He was a civil engineering student at the University of California, Berkeley, but said, "I really want to make music my living." With a straight face, he boasted that he had "no professional training," and while Simon told him that he couldn't sing or dance, William won America's heart by smiling and declaring that he gave his best, and had "no regrets at all." He wound up making the talk show rounds and even scored a record deal. Having released three albums, *Inspiration, Hung for the Holidays,* and *Miracle: Happy Summer from William Hung*, William continues to appear in commercials and other spots proving that *Idol* can make dreams come true, even without a coveted golden ticket.

AVEN MOORE

Little Orphan Annie never sounded like this. Clad in purple with a headband straight out of 1983, Aven Moore of Harrisburg, Virginia, put his all into "Tomorrow"—including a final note he held for what seemed like an eternity—but there would be no sunshine in the form of a gold-colored piece of paper. Scratching his head, Simon simply called it "bizarrely dreadful."

MARY ROACH

She seemed normal at first—composed on camera talking to Ryan in the waiting room, describing her voice as "pop rock meets Broadway and jazz R&B"—but signs of the zany were there. Then Mary Roach, a nineteen-year-old cosmetology student from Virginia who said she was going to change her name to Mary Guilbeaux if she made it to Hollywood, launched into Carole King's "I Feel the Earth Move," and it all went downhill from there. Simon said she couldn't sing a note and her voice was weird. Mary countered that weird can be original. She then talked about the voices in her head, complimented guest judge Mark McGrath, and told Paula that she looked thinner in person. In the hallway, Mary hurled her share of expletives at Simon, Randy, and McGrath (even though she had just called him a "hottie"), but Paula was spared. The audience, however, was not as Mary departed with one last song. The voices should have told her to stop.

GENERAL LARRY PLATT

The rules say *Idol*'s cutoff age is twenty-eight, but that didn't stop Atlanta's General Larry Platt from auditioning in season nine. The sixty-three-year-old civil rights activist and rapper had a message for America's youth, and while he may have been ineligible to compete, he nonetheless became legendary as he unveiled his original composition, "Pants on the Ground," complete with break-dancing moves, for the judges panel (including guest Mary J. Blige). After the segment aired, it became the talk of the nation as talk show host Jimmy Fallon did a parody of the song dressed as Neil Young, and even a U.S. congressman made reference to it during a filibuster. "Pants on the Ground" sold 116,000 downloads, peaking at number forty-six on the *Billboard* charts (Simon predicted it would be a hit). Larry Platt got his own fan page on Facebook, appeared on *The View* to perform the track, and was invited back to the season nine finale in 2010. Funny as he may be, he's no fool.

BIKINI GIRL

Her name is Katrina Darrell, but after her season eight audition, she would forever be known as Bikini Girl. Clad in only a two-piece and heels, she professed her love for Ryan, revealing that she had picked out their kids' names and that they would "make out" once she got her golden ticket. Katrina launched into Mariah Carey's "Vision of Love," but it was clear Simon was sold before she sang the second line, since he immediately said yes. Guest judge Kara DioGuardi? Not so much. "You don't have the chops to sing that song," she offered matter-of-factly after demonstrating how it should be sung. Katrina fired back that Kara's demonstration was no better. Kara could only compliment the girl's derriere. It didn't matter; Katrina got her ticket and a chance to smooch Ryan. Though she didn't make it to the finals, Katrina returned to serenade America with her best Mariah Carey for the finale. Alas, she was upstaged, once again, by Kara, who not only sang her butt off, but unveiled her own bikini body.

NICK MITCHELL/NORMAN GENTLE

When we were first introduced to "Norman Gentle" (aka Nick Mitchell) at the New York City tryouts for season eight, nobody was sure if his audition was for real or a joke. Wearing a shiny disco shirt with a red headband, the Connecticut native left the judges confused with his rendition of "And I Am Telling You I'm Not Going" from the musical *Dreamgirls*. It turned out Nick had some vocal chops, but what was with the strange alter ego? Randy took forever to decide on a "yes" vote, Kara was banging her fist on the desk, and Simon told Nick, "I want to kick you between the legs but I think you'd like it." Nick fired back, in character: "The way you like it when Seacrest does it?" That one moment propelled Nick Mitchell into *AI* history, earning him a golden ticket to Hollywood. He made it all the way to the top thirty-six, and even got a prominent spot singing his signature song during the season eight finale. He made an encore appearance on season nine, when he joined William Hung and other members of the wacky club for a Simon send-off song with Dane Cook. Nick/Norman can now be seen regularly on the *Wendy Williams Show* offering his own *American Idol* commentary.

EARLY FAN FAVORITES

ALEX LAMBERT SEASON NINE: He was a natural talent with a booming voice but little stage presence, which may account for why the North Richland Hills, Texas, native was sent home one week shy of the top twelve. Fans were so outraged by Alex's elimination that that they started an online petition, and as a result of the public outcry, he was cast as the sixth housemate on the live Internet series *If I Can Dream*.

LILLY SCOTT SEASON NINE: She didn't quite fit the *American Idol* mold, but that's exactly what viewers liked about Littleton, Colorado, native Lilly Scott, whose quirky take on The Beatles endeared the gray-haired wonder to millions.

JACKIE TOHN SEASON EIGHT: Actress, comedienne, singer, would-be Idol . . . As entertainers go, L.A.'s Jackie Tohn had it all, including a killer voice. But when her kooky dance moves threw Simon for a loop, the audience followed and Jackie was eliminated one week into the top thirty-six. No matter, a year later she was back on television with a guest spot on TNT's *Memphis Beat*.

TATIANA DEL TORO SEASON EIGHT: Between the crying and cackling, Tatiana Del Toro was the Hollywood Week hopeful who annoyed all to no end. While fellow contestants and judges alike didn't know quite what to make of the Puerto Rican auditioner, there was no doubt she had one performance perfected: her rendition of "Saving All My Love for You."

JOSIAH LEMING SEASON SEVEN: Another unlikely *Idol* candidate came by way of hopeful Josiah Leming, who advanced on the strength of his original music, unique voice, and tragic backstory of living out of his car. Fortunately, his homelessness was short-lived. Though he narrowly missed the top twenty-four, the emo Josiah was offered a record deal with Warner Bros. Records soon after.

AYLA BROWN SEASON FIVE: Ayla's reputation preceded her top twenty-four showing. Not only was she an accomplished NCAA basketball player by the time she auditioned, but her father was also a noted U.S. politician (now a senator from Massachusetts) and her mother a local news anchor. No wonder she followed in the family's footsteps and secured herself a public career as a correspondent for CBS' *The Early Show*.

MARIO VAZQUEZ SEASON FOUR: The Bronx-born singer impressed the judges early on with his R&B grooves and stage-ready moves, so much so that the compliments sent him packing—by his own choice! The top twelve contender left the competition early and signed a deal with Clive Davis's Arista Records.

FRENCHIE DAVIS SEASON TWO: She was a girl with big dreams, and though she never made it past the top thirty, Frenchie Davis did eventually make a name for herself on a big stage: Broadway. Shortly after her *Idol* dismissal, Frenchie landed a role in *Rent*, which led to future castings in touring productions of *Dreamgirls* and *Ain't Misbehavin'* alongside season two winner Ruben Studdard.

ALEXIS LOPEZ SEASON ONE: Simon Cowell was smitten with this season one beauty, who made it to the semifinals, was voted out, and then given a second chance (courtesy of Cowell) during the wild card round. Alas, Alexis was cut loose one week shy of the top ten, and the rest is Kelly Clarkson history . . .

IDOL
— BY THE —
NUMBERS

3

Guinness Book of World Records, *for most votes received in one night.*

794,817

Number of people who have auditioned.

1,794

Number of contestants who have been invited to Hollywood Week.

67

Number of cities visited over the past 10 seasons.

624 MILLION

Highest number of votes per season: season 8

4,050,015,362

Number of votes received. (Yes, more than 4 billion!)

To date, American Idols have collectively sold more than 45 million albums and 115 million single song downloads in the United States alone. Artists launched from the show have achieved 245 no. 1's on the Billboard Charts, 7 Grammy Awards, 1 Oscar, and numerous American Music Awards, Academy of Country Music Awards, Country Music Association Awards, MTV's VMA Awards, People's Choice Awards, Teen Choice Awards, Billboard Awards, and CMT Awards.

AMERICAN IDOL № 1's
by CONTESTANT

56	KELLY CLARKSON
48	CARRIE UNDERWOOD
36	CHRIS DAUGHTRY (DAUGHTRY)
24	FANTASIA
16	RUBEN STUDDARD
13	JENNIFER HUDSON
11	CLAY AIKEN
10	MANDISA
8	KIMBERLEY LOCKE
7	JOSH GRACIN
7	JORDIN SPARKS
6	DAVID COOK
5	ADAM LAMBERT
4	DAVID ARCHULETA
4	KELLIE PICKLER
4	ELLIOTT YAMIN
3	KRIS ALLEN
3	TAYLOR HICKS
2	BO BICE
2	BUCKY COVINGTON
2	BLAKE LEWIS
2	CHRIS SLIGH
1	PARIS BENNETT
1	JASON CASTRO
1	DIANA DEGARMO
1	LEE DEWYZE
1	TAMYRA GRAY
1	WILLIAM HUNG

CHAPTER 9: **SEASON FIVE**

AMERICAN IDOL TURNED a corner in season five. Having discovered bona fide stars like Kelly Clarkson, Clay Aiken, and Carrie Underwood, netting sales of 33 million worldwide, it was able to command the largest TV audience the show had ever seen. More than 500 million votes were cast that season as Taylor Hicks and Katharine McPhee vied for the title, but plenty more contestants became household names. Chris Daughtry even went on to become the third most successful Idol ever.

Who could forget Kellie Pickler's schooling on modern American cuisine—that's a silent *L* in "salmon" and "calamari" is another word for squid—all live on TV! Or how about Kevin Covais, who was declared the group's "sex symbol" one week, then nicknamed Chicken Little on another. He, along with Lisa Tucker and Paris Bennett, was one of three contestants who had yet to turn eighteen but who displayed vocal chops far beyond their years. Season five also had Bucky Covington, a good ol' country boy from North Carolina with an unmistakable twang and a twin brother in the audience who would instantly prompt a double take. You could say the same of resident heartthrob Ace Young, who impressed early on with his falsetto on songs like Michael Jackson's "Butterflies" and Daniel Bedingfield's "If You're Not the One."

But in the end, it came down to four singers, each with an entirely different vocal style, and one of whom went on to become a rocker sensation: Chris Daughtry. The rocker from North Carolina exhibited honesty, humility, and passion in each performance, no matter how hard the song—and some, like Creed's "What If," definitely pushed *Idol* to its guitar-shredding max. Then you had Elliott Yamin. Dubbed the "funky white boy" by Paula Abdul, he could make hearts melt with

his velvety-smooth delivery on classics by Ray Charles and Donny Hathaway. Rounding out the runners-up was Katharine McPhee, a stunner both in beauty and vocal brawn. The Great American Songbook was her forte, and it included the Judy Garland classic (chosen by Simon) "Somewhere Over the Rainbow," which garnered a reaction so nice she sang it twice.

All three came close (with less than one percentage point separating the top three), but no one could unseat the powerhouse that was Taylor Hicks, who called on his Soul Patrol to vote and they came through big time. "The silver fox," as Ryan described him on one occasion, was known to hoot, holler, and shake his thing, but it wasn't just showmanship that clinched the *Idol* crown. Taylor's unique singing style swept the nation and reaffirmed a statement Randy had made during the top twenty-four: "There's never been anyone on this show that's like you."

And even though *Idol* had been on the air for nearly half a decade, season five still had a few firsts. It introduced the send-off song, Daniel Powter's "Bad Day," which became a number one hit for the Warner Bros. Records artist. It was the first time Bruce Springsteen had authorized the use of one of his songs on the show—the iconic "Dancing in the Dark," chosen for Taylor by music business veteran Clive Davis. It also marked the first season to broadcast in high-definition. But as some things changed, others remained the same. Randy still flagrantly abused the words "dog" and "dude," Ryan continued to spar with Simon, and Simon's relationship with Paula entered a new dimension of faux frostiness when she requested to sit on the opposite end of the judges' table during semifinals. In the end, they came back together, though not without a hand or two in somebody's face, and it was one happy, dysfunctional family yet again . . .

CLASS *of* 06

SEASON 5 YEARBOOK

"You're so confident, Paris. You're like a performing little doll. Wind her up and off you go! Very good." —Simon Cowell

PARIS BENNETT
"High School Student"

KEVIN COVAIS
"High School Student"

BUCKY COVINGTON
"Mechanic"

CHRIS DAUGHTRY
"Car Dealership Service Adviser"

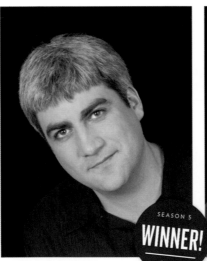

SEASON 5
WINNER!
2002

TAYLOR HICKS
"Musician-Singer"

MANDISA HUNDLEY
"Backup Singer"

"Taylor potentially has the most charisma, which is a very, very important part of being a star." —David Foster

MELISSA MCGHEE

"Law Firm Assistant"

KATHARINE MCPHEE

"Singer-Actress"

SEASON 5

RUNNER-UP

2002

KELLIE PICKLER

"Waitress"

LISA TUCKER

"High School Student"

ELLIOTT YAMIN

"Pharmacy Clerk"

ACE YOUNG

"Singer"

WINNER'S CIRCLE

Looking back with the season five champ

You're from Alabama—how did you end up in Las Vegas for *Idol* auditions?

Taylor Hicks: Hurricane Katrina had just hit my hometown and I had a free voucher to fly anywhere in the country. I went to Las Vegas because I'd never been there and heard it's a fun place to go. I was just hanging out until my brother called at midnight to tell me *Idol* auditions were the next day. I had nothing better to do, so I showed up at 4:00 a.m., got in line with some very interesting people, and started rolling with it.

Song choice was key in your victory. How did you decide what to sing?

TH: I tried to pick songs that meant something to me. If you can connect to the songs emotionally, then you can communicate them to the people. I learned that through years of performing. I auditioned with "A Change Is Gonna Come" because I felt a change was coming for me. Then during the competition, the key was to be visually stimulating and to pick songs that people can sing along to when they're not watching you. You have to make sure you choose popular numbers. I also asked them to allow me the freedom to write the last thirty seconds to each song. I knew those endings were big as well.

When you whipped out your harmonica during the top twenty-four judgment, you became the first contestant to play an instrument on the show.

TH: They told me they would send me home if I did it and I said, "OK, I'll take the risk." During the elevator ride, I decided it was now or never. It was my make-or-break moment and I played my harmonica all the way while walking to see the judges. They didn't know what to think. They never had a contestant with such a strong will to do well in that competition. It was premeditated.

What other winning strategies did you employ?

TH: There's a humidity issue in CBS studios. It's all re-processed air, so by the time you get to the stage with the smoke and the dryness and the air-conditioning, the richness of your voice could be gone. So I spent a lot of time in the bathroom—the one place in that building where you could keep your voice moist, if you could stand the smell. Other than that, because I couldn't use instruments, I had to look beyond to find ways to stand out each week and be different.

What's your take on the judges?

TH: What's great about the show is each of the judges represented something: Paula was the performer, Randy was the musician, and Simon was the label head. You have to take what Simon says with a grain of salt. Personally, I think he's a perfect person for dealing with pop music. He was representative of someone who would run a label or be in A&R for a record label.

TAYLOR HICKS

* **HOMETOWN:** Birmingham, Alabama

* **AUDITION SONG:** "A Change Is Gonna Come" by Sam Cooke

* **WORDS TO LIVE BY:** *"You're like every dad who's ever gotten drunk at a wedding. I'm being positive! It's a compliment! Every dad has gotten drunk at a wedding and gone onstage and sung. The difference is you can sing."* Simon

LIFE AFTER IDOL: Season five's gray-haired wonder had long honed his vocal chops at local bars and honky-tonks, so it came as no surprise that Taylor Hicks hit the ground running soon after his *Idol* win. Indeed, Taylor em-barked on two simultaneous tours in the summer of 2006, playing arenas nightly with the top ten and sometimes his own late-night club gigs, where fellow finalists like Elliott Yamin, Chris Daughtry, Ace Young, and Bucky Covington were known to make surprise appearances.

Having won a recording contract with Arista Records, Taylor spent much of the following fall in the studio with renowned producer Matt Serletic. His self-titled debut was released in December, landing at the number-one spot, thanks to support from the ever-loyal Soul Patrol. The following year, Taylor released his autobiography, *Heart Full of Soul: An Inspirational Memoir About Finding Your Voice and Finding Your Way*. Taking the book's title to heart, he and Arista went their separate ways, but Taylor continued on his musical path, releasing a collection of his early works in 2009 and an independent studio album, *The Distance*, in 2009.

In the years since his *Idol* victory, Taylor has also taken to the theater, appearing in the national touring production of *Grease* as Teen Angel. And like the season five summer trek, he's once again performing a double header, offering a solo set following his act three bow.

KATHARINE MCPHEE

* **HOMETOWN:** Sherman Oaks, California

* **AUDITION SONG:** "God Bless the Child" by Billie Holiday

* **WORDS TO LIVE BY:** *"Absolutely brilliant. You are really good. . . . What a natural gift. One hundred percent you are what this competition is all about."* —Randy

LIFE AFTER IDOL: It was evident from day one that Katharine McPhee, a stunning beauty and undeniable talent, was poised for greatness. And after coming in second to Taylor Hicks, she wasted no time reaching for the stars, starting with her gold-certified self-titled debut, which entered the *Billboard* album chart at number two upon its release in January 2007. It would be three years before Katharine—or Kat, as she's affectionately known—would release a follow-up, but *Unbroken* was well worth the wait and featured a song that gained new popularity just as *Idol*'s season nine kicked off; the song "Terrified," cowritten by Kara DioGuardi and featured on Kat's album as a duet with singer-songwriter Jason Reeves (and later *Chuck* star Zachari Levi), was performed by Didi Benami on Hollywood Week and sales shot up immediately.

Making the most out of her *Idol* experience, Katharine also stayed close to season five mentors Andrea Bocelli and David Foster, collaborating with both for various albums and performances, including the PBS all-star tribute *Hit Man: David Foster & Friends*. But her appearances on the screen were not limited to the musical kind. In 2007, Kat appeared as

herself on ABC's *Ugly Betty*, and a year later she landed the part of Anna Faris's sorority sister in *The House Bunny.* Guest stints on TV shows like *CSI: NY* and *Community* came next as Kat continued to pursue acting. But singing remains closest to Kat's heart, along with family, which includes her husband, Nick, and vocal coach mother, Peisha. Bringing the three together is Kat's latest album: *Christmas Is a Time . . . to Say I Love You.*

ELLIOTT YAMIN

* **HOMETOWN:** Richmond, Virginia

* **AUDITION SONG:** "A Song for You" by Donny Hathaway

* **WORDS TO LIVE BY:** *"There are so many things that I adore about you, Elliott, and one of them is that you are such a breath of fresh air to this business because you are humble, you are unstated, and you know you're great, but you have that careless reckless abandon about you. You know how to pick the right songs for your voice and stay true to who you are. I think you're fantastic and you keep growing."* —Paula

* **LIFE AFTER *IDOL*:** No stranger to defying the odds, having lived with 90 percent hearing loss in his right ear for much of his life and as a diabetic since the age of sixteen, the velvety-voiced Elliott Yamin opted to take the independent route following his third-place finish. He

signed a publishing deal with Sony/ATV in December 2006, then a record deal with "virtual label" Hickory Records and saw his self-titled first album debut at number three on the *Billboard* album chart, thanks, in large part, to the radio hit "Wait for You," which he performed on season six's top three results show.

Sales of his album skyrocketed afterward, landing Elliott in the exclusive "gold" club and allowing him opportunities rarely afforded to *Idol* finalists. Among them: a nationwide headlining tour, which included a performance on "A Capitol Fourth," broadcast on PBS on Independence Day; international shows in far-off lands like the Philippines and Japan; and TV cameos, such as when he played himself on soap opera *The Bold and the Beautiful* in the summer of 2007.

That's not to say that music took a backseat. Elliot spent much of 2008 and 2009 doing little else but recording, writing, and collaborating. He had released two holiday albums by then and was working on his much-anticipated follow-up, *Fight for Love*, leaving just enough time to appear on Taylor Hicks's *The Distance* (singing a cover of Bobby Womack's "Woman's Gotta Have It") as well as *Randy Jackson's Music Club, Vol. 1*, on which he duets with Katharine McPhee.

Where there is a spare moment, Elliott devotes it to charity work. Through Idol Gives Back's antimalaria initiative, he's visited Angola twice, first with Fantasia in 2008 and again in 2010 with Kara DioGuardi. In 2009, he secured a $100,000 grant from ExxonMobil to help build the Saint Isabel Orphanage and School in the city of Luanda. A year later, Elliott returned to the African nation to check on its progress. Back home (which the Virginia native now calls Los Angeles), he's been involved as an advocate and fund-raiser for a variety of diabetes-related programs and organizations, including the Juvenile Diabetes Research Foundation and the World Diabetes Congress, for which he was guest speaker in 2009. Elliott's third album is slated for release in 2011.

CHRIS DAUGHTRY

* **HOMETOWN:** McLeansville, North Carolina

* **AUDITION SONG:** "The Letter" by Joe Cocker (originally by The Box Tops)

* **WORDS TO LIVE BY:** *"I've been wowed by you from day one . . . your artistry, what you pick to sing. It's as if you've been doing it for the longest time."* —Paula

* **LIFE AFTER *IDOL*:** *American Idol*'s highest-selling male alumnus is the gravelly voiced Chris Daughtry, who came to the competition a disenchanted service rep at a Honda dealer and exited in fourth place as a shining pillar of rock 'n' roll's vitality. He saw one of his musical dreams come true during the season five finale, when Chris got to sing with his own idols, the band Live, but within six months of that performance, his own band, Daughtry, had sold more than 1 million copies of its self-titled debut and reached number one on the *Billboard* album charts. (It's since moved more than 4.5 million units.)

In fact, arena-ready rockers like "It's Not Over" and "Home" were radio staples for the best part of three years (the latter even becoming the season six elimination theme song) during

which Chris toured the country several times over and garnered no less than four Grammy nominations. Having cowritten many of the tracks on *Daughtry*, Chris earned the respect of the music industry and became an in-demand collaborator, appearing on songs by the likes of Theory of a Deadman, Lifehouse, and Carlos Santana. Daughtry's second album, 2009's *Leave This Town*, was another hit, selling more than 1 million copies.

On television, Chris could be seen regularly both on network and cable, be it a cameo on *CSI: NY*, performances on *Dick Clark's New Year's Rockin' Eve with Ryan Seacrest*, the Super Bowl XLIV preshow, or his three return appearances on *Idol*.

And while Daughtry's talent, both the person and the band, is undeniable, its success—more than 1 million albums sold and counting—is simply baffling. In fact, he's the third-most-successful Idol, led only by Kelly Clarkson and Carrie Underwood. Of course, it's not just about selling records and rocking the stages of the world, and when he's not making music, Chris is a devoted husband and proud father of four, most recently to twins.

PARIS BENNETT

✳ **HOMETOWN:** Fayetteville, Georgia

✳ **AUDITION SONGS:** "Cowboy Take Me Away" by The Dixie Chicks; "Take Five" by Paul Desmond

✳ **WORDS TO LIVE BY:** *"Maybe I just didn't realize how young she is . . . to be able to have that kind of depth and power in her voice was just shocking. This girl has got an enormous career ahead of her."* —Barry Manilow

✳ **LIFE AFTER *IDOL*:** Paris Bennett comes from a long line of exceptional singers, starting with her grandmother then her mother, the former lead singer of Sounds of Blackness, so it's no wonder the then-seventeen-year-old was born with super-powered pipes. Paris had hints of old jazz and classic R&B in her singing style, popular sounds from way before her time, and the judges took notice immediately. Still, weeks of impressive performances couldn't save her from a fifth-place elimination. What came next was a slew of television appearances and, in 2007, her debut album, the aptly upbeat *Princess P*, titled after the nickname Ryan Seacrest was so fond of and featuring collaborations with Rodney Jerkins and fellow season five finalist Kevin Covais. In 2008, Paris released *A Royal Christmas*, which featured modernized versions of Christmas staples like "Lil' Drummer Boy" and "Deck the Halls." That same year, she gave birth to a daughter, Egypt, telling *People* magazine, "Man, does she have lungs on her. I guess she's gearing up to be the next American Idol."

KELLIE PICKLER

✳ **HOMETOWN:** Albemarle, North Carolina

✳ **AUDITION SONGS:** "Since U Been Gone" by Kelly Clarkson; "A Broken Wing" by Martina McBride

✳ **WORDS TO LIVE BY:** *"You're unpretentious, you don't have the diva attitude, you have the likability factor up the scale to the highest level, and that's gonna carry you."* —Paula

✳ **LIFE AFTER *IDOL*:** Bubbly, blonde, precocious, and hilarious (the latter often unintentional), Southern belle Kellie Pickler charmed the pants off the judges—even an extra-crabby Simon Cowell—and the TV audience, and managed to make it all the way up to sixth place in one of the toughest talent pools to grace the *Idol* stage. So what happened next? Plenty, as Kellie went on to become a country star in her own right.

Signed to 19 Recordings/BNA Records soon after the *Idol* summer tour kicked off, Kellie's debut album, *Small Town Girl*, was released in October 2006, landing the top spot on *Billboard*'s Top Country Albums chart and entering the *Billboard* 200 at number nine. Her first single, "Red High Heels" (which Kellie cowrote), and its accompanying music video, was a stunner, and in due time, Kellie received nominations from highly respected institutions like the Academy of Country Music and the Country Music Association. The accolades didn't stop there. In 2008, Kellie released her self-titled second album, debuting in the exact same chart positions as her first. That year, she

also went up against Taylor Swift for several Best New Artist awards.

As Kellie's popularity grew through country radio hits and several national tours, including opening slots for Rascal Flatts, Sugarland, Brad Paisley, and Taylor Swift, so did her charity work. FOX viewers got a repeat dose of Kellie's legendary ditziness when she faced a group of kids half her age on the game show *Are You Smarter Than a Fifth Grader?* Guaranteed $25,000 for her charity of choice (American Red Cross and AARP's Grandparenting Program), she gingerly accepted the humiliation of having to answer no. Kellie is active in animal rights issues and was named World's Sexiest Vegetarian by PETA in 2009. She's also participated in no less than three USO tours, the most recent in 2010 taking her close to the front lines of the war in Iraq and Kuwait. That summer, Kellie also announced her engagement to longtime boyfriend, songwriter Kyle Jacobs.

ACE YOUNG

⁑ **HOMETOWN:** Boulder, Colorado

⁑ **AUDITION SONGS:** "Walking Away" by Craig David; "Swear It Again" by Westlife

⁑ **WORDS TO LIVE BY:** *"You definitely are a star. You're working the camera, you're working the room . . . You really got it going on, plus, the most important thing, you can really sing!"* —Randy

⁑ **LIFE AFTER *IDOL*:** Dapper and charming with a soulful falsetto that made Paula Abdul swoon every single time, Ace Young was season five's resident heartthrob, a duty that wasn't rescinded after his seventh-place finish. To the contrary, Ace made *People* magazine's list of hottest bachelors less than a month after the finale, an honor that would lead to TV stints (like playing a karaoke singer—alongside season six's Brandon Rogers—on FOX's *Bones* in 2008) and eventually a starring role on Broadway.

Indeed, though Ace released his self-titled debut in 2008, the theater is where he's spent much of his post-*Idol* days—and nights. That same year, he played Danny Zuko in the national touring production of *Grease*, then landed the role of Berger in the Broadway revival of *Hair*, where he was joined by cast member and season three alum Diana DeGarmo. But working on music—whether his own or with friends—remains a top priority in Ace's professional life. In fact, he helped write the chorus to Chris Daughtry's massive hit, "It's Not Over," a collaboration that would net Ace a Grammy nod for Best Rock Song and land him in the exclusive club of Idol nominees.

BUCKY COVINGTON

⁑ **HOMETOWN:** Rockingham, North Carolina

⁑ **AUDITION SONG:** "Take It Easy" by The Eagles

⁑ **WORDS TO LIVE BY:** *"I like you because I think you're a very sincere guy. I don't think you're playing as we see sometimes—you are what you are, and I like that."* —Simon

⁑ **LIFE AFTER *IDOL*:** Season five's "good ol' country boy" contestant made every performance feel like a Bucky Covington concert, and the cheers continued well past his eighth-place

bow. Seeing a down-home vibe to the talented cowboy, Bucky signed with Lyric Street Records, home to Rascal Flatts and SHeDaisy, and released his self-titled first album in 2007. It debuted at number one on the Country Album charts, eventually producing three country radio hits. Bucky's second album, *I'm Alright*, featuring a cover of Nickelback's "Gotta Be Somebody," was released in September 2010.

Embracing the many new experiences that have come out of the show, he's appeared at *Idol* camp and the opening of Walt Disney World's American Idol Experience, and even the occasional unexpected booking, like when he appeared in 2009's *Hannah Montana: The Movie*, playing guitar in labelmate Billy Ray Cyrus's band.

MANDISA HUNDLEY

⁑ **HOMETOWN:** Antioch, Tennessee

⁑ **AUDITION SONG:** "Fallin'" by Alicia Keys

⁑ **WORDS TO LIVE BY:** *"Mandisa is one of those girls that have range. She can sing from the bottom to the top without any trouble. She's like one of a kind."* —Barry Manilow

⁑ **LIFE AFTER *IDOL*:** She sang the gospel as well as she preached it, so it's no wonder Mandisa stayed true to her own path and became a successful Christian artist. A year after her ninth-place finish, Mandisa released her autobiography, *IdolEyes*, in conjunction with her debut album, *True Beauty*, which entered the *Bill-*

board Top Christian Albums chart at number one, the first time a female artist had done so in the chart's twenty-seven-year history. Another first: The album received a Grammy nomination for Best Pop/Contemporary Gospel Album and has since sold more than 150,000 copies.

Dividing days and nights between stage shows and time spent in the studio, where she would record a Christmas album (*It's Christmas*, released in 2008) and her second full-length album, Mandisa also managed to lose more than seventy-five pounds since March 2009, which inspired her to name that sophomore album *Freedom*.

LISA TUCKER

* **HOMETOWN:** Anaheim, California

* **AUDITION SONG:** "One Moment in Time" by Whitney Houston

* **WORDS TO LIVE BY:** *"Sixteen-year-old Lisa Tucker—one of the greatest contestants I've ever seen on* American Idol." —Ryan

* **LIFE AFTER *IDOL*:** After her audition, Simon Cowell declared Lisa Tucker "the best sixteen-year-old we've had through this whole competition," and even with all that pressure, you never saw the girl sweat. That's because the R&B princess had the confidence of a pro with the chops to match, albeit it may not have been her time. Still, Lisa made the summer tour and went on to book several TV appearances, including recurring roles on Nickelodeon's *Zoey 101* and the CW's *The Game,* as well as a stint playing herself on *The OC.* She made her share of musical cameos as well, appearing on Dionne Warwick's 2006 album, *My Friends & Me,* and performing in 2008 for U.S. troops stationed in Europe.

KEVIN COVAIS

* **HOMETOWN:** Levittown, New York

* **AUDITION SONG:** "You Raise Me Up" by Josh Groban

* **WORDS TO LIVE BY:** *"I think anyone over the age of eighty would love you."* —Simon

* **LIFE AFTER *IDOL*:** He may not have made the touring top ten, but Kevin Covais—dubbed Chicken Little by his pal Paris Bennett, which was soon adopted by Ryan Seacrest and thus, the world—stands among *Idol*'s most memorable contestants. Maybe it's because Paula called him a sex symbol, or perhaps it's due to the successful acting career he's nurtured since his season five exit. In 2006, Kevin costarred in the comedy *College* alongside Drake Bell. Following that appearance, he landed a role in the movie *Labor Pains,* starring Lindsay Lohan, and made his small-screen debut in *Ghost Whis-*

perer. Singing remains a love of Kevin's and he's made more than his share of appearances, both locally and beyond.

MELISSA MCGHEE

* **HOMETOWN:** Tampa, Florida

* **AUDITION SONG:** "Words to Live By" by LeAnn Rimes

* **WORDS TO LIVE BY:** *"I'm just a fun-loving girl from Florida. I have a great heart and music is my passion."*—Melissa McGhee

* **LIFE AFTER *IDOL*:** She made it through Hollywood Week, past the top twenty-four, and on to her final stop, the top twelve, and upon returning home to Tampa, Melissa McGhee was hailed as a local celebrity for having outsung tens of thousands of hopefuls. Since that fateful day in 2006, she's kept her *Idol* family close, appearing in a tour with fellow alums Diana DeGarmo, Justin Guarini, Vonzell Solomon, Mikalah Gordon, and Rickey Smith, among others.

Greatest Hits

TROUBLE

TAYLOR HICKS

MARCH 28, 2006

With a spot on the summer tour on the line, Birmingham, Alabama's gray-haired wonder Taylor Hicks truly proved his Idol potential when he delivered a from-the-gut rendition of Ray LaMontagne's great lament during Hits of the 2000s Week. The top ten performance became an instant classic, carrying Hicks—and his Soul Patrol army—to victory.

SOMEWHERE OVER THE RAINBOW

KATHARINE McPHEE

MAY 17, 2006

It was down to the wire, but the final three was all about Katharine McPhee. The Sherman Oaks, California, stunner had already dazzled with her delivery of Whitney Houston's "I Have Nothing" (prompting Simon Cowell to apologize the following night for having called it "cabaret"), and impressed with her version of K. T. Tunstall's "Black Horse and the Cherry Tree," but it was her performance of Judy Garland's signature song that sent Katharine into overdrive.

I'M THE ONLY ONE

KELLIE PICKLER

MARCH 7, 2006

With her cute-as-a-button drawl and powerful country-flavored pipes, the great blonde hope from Albemarle, North Carolina, endeared herself to *Idol* viewers—and the judges—early on. Look no further than her final stop on the top twenty-four, when Kellie's turn at Melissa Etheridge's "I'm the Only One" prompted Simon to label her "a naughty little minx." "A *whaaaat?*" Kellie asked, not sure if he'd just insulted her. To the contrary, Simon was and remains one of her biggest fans.

I WALK THE LINE

CHRIS DAUGHTRY

MARCH 21, 2006

Out to prove he wasn't your grandma's *Idol* contestant, on the second week of the top twelve, Chris Daughtry turned an iconic 1950s hit, Johnny Cash's "I Walk the Line," into a moody alternative rock number that showed he meant business. The judges applauded his twist, with Simon Cowell going so far as to praise Chris for being the first *Idol* hopeful "who's actually refused to compromise." Indeed, the weeks that followed only affirmed Cowell's confidence in North Carolina native who would go on to be the best-selling graduate of *Idol's* school of rock.

A SONG FOR YOU

ELLIOTT YAMIN

APRIL 25, 2006

Season five's other dark horse, Elliott Yamin from Richmond, Virginia, auditioned for *Idol* with this Donny Hathaway/Leon Russell soul classic, but the footage never aired. He brought it back with a passionate vengeance during Great Love Songs Week, moving Paula Abdul to tears and prompting Simon to declare the top three finalist part of a "vocal master class."

FATHER FIGURE

ACE YOUNG

FEBRUARY 22, 2006

A handsome Ace Young chose George Michael's sultry "Father Figure" as his first introduction to America. Simon called it "a brilliant choice of song" and promised Ace he'd "sail through to the next round, which he did for eight more weeks.

IDOL ROCKS

AFTER BO BICE KICKED DOWN THE PROVERBIAL ROCK 'N' ROLL DOOR ON SEASON FOUR, A STRING OF HEAVY-MINDED HOPEFULS FOLLOWED, TURNING THE *IDOL* VOLUME UP TO ELEVEN. FROM LONG HAIR TO NO HAIR, 1980S POWER BALLADS TO ARENA ANTHEMS, THERE'S NOTHING THESE SEVEN SIZZLING ROCKERS CAN'T SLAY . . .

CHRIS DAUGHTRY: He may be *Idol's* bestselling rocker, but Chris Daughtry from McLeansville, North Carolina, had his own stint in the bottom two while competing in season five (after singing Louis Armstrong's eternally optimistic "What a Wonderful World"). Fortunately, there were far more standing ovation–worthy bows by the former car mechanic. From Bon Jovi's "Wanted Dead or Alive" to Creed's "What If" to Fuel's "Hemorrhage (in My Hands)," and on two multiplatinum albums since his fourth-place finish, it goes to show: When raw and grungy rock is your calling card, stick to it.

BO BICE: The show's pioneering rocker brought monster classic-rock riffs to the *Idol* stage (long before contestants were allowed to play instruments) and, in no time, went from being a straggly, bell-bottomed hopeful to performing with some of his own idols. Singing "Sweet Home Alabama" at the season four finale with Lynyrd Skynyrd as his backing band was a high point for the Helena, Alabama, native, but for his fans, the seminal Southern rallying cry was just the last in a string of stellar performances that not only got Bo to second place, but also forever endeared him to the hearts of rock loving *Idol* worshipers.

DAVID COOK: The first contestant to rock a six-string on the *Idol* stage is also among the show's most venerated. From the very start of season seven, the Blue Springs, Missouri, charmer delivered world-class vocals to songs completely reimagined. From Michael Jackson's "Billie Jean" to Mariah Carey's "Always Be My Baby," no matter what the theme, nothing in the pop world seemed to make the lifelong rocker sweat—not even eventual runner-up David Archuleta.

CONSTANTINE MAROULIS: Bo's season four partner in long-haired crime was New York rocker Constantine Maroulis, whose brooding stare and powerful pipes earned him the honor of being among the show's first punks-turned-hunks. His shining moment came during the top eight, when Constantine's spot-on version of Queen's "Bohemian Rhapsody" became an instant *Idol* classic. He didn't last long after (only two more weeks, to be exact), but the memories have endured for years since.

ADAM LAMBERT: Flipping the rock 'n' roll formula on its glittered and guy-linered head, season eight runner-up Adam Lambert forever redefined the art of the dramatic performance with his *Idol* arc. From a moody, Middle Eastern reinterpretation of an Americana classic like Johnny Cash's "Ring of Fire" to his showstopping twist on Tears for Fears' early 1980s hit "Mad World," every song Adam touched turned to glam, carrying the San Diego native all the way to the finale and far beyond.

ALLISON IRAHETA: With a rock-ready rasp that was way beyond her years (sixteen at the time of season eight auditions), Allison Iraheta could handle classic vocals that were decades ahead of her time (like Foghat's "Slow Ride") with the same confidence delivered on songs she grew up with, like No Doubt's "Don't Speak." No matter which way you slice it, this Latina looker is fierce!

CARLY SMITHSON: Tattooed and fierce with a wail that needs no amplification, Irish transplant Carly Smithson would tear the roof off the *Idol* studio week after week. She first made her rock mark with a rousing rendition of Heart's "Crazy on You," but the octave-defying stunt work was just getting started as she made her way through season seven. Carly is probably best remembered for her spine-chilling take on Bonnie Tyler's "Total Eclipse of the Heart," which ended up winning the hearts of millions.

American Idol

SEASON 5

BACKSTAGE PASS

10

CHAPTER 10: **STYLE**

10

IDOLS' GREATEST MAKEOVERS

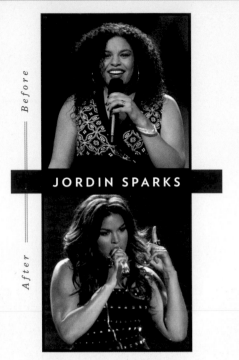

Before

JORDIN SPARKS

After

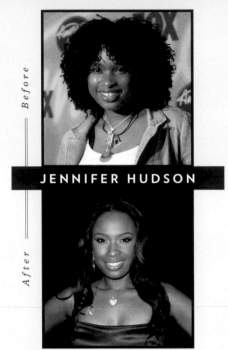

Before

JENNIFER HUDSON

After

Before

KATHARINE McPHEE

After

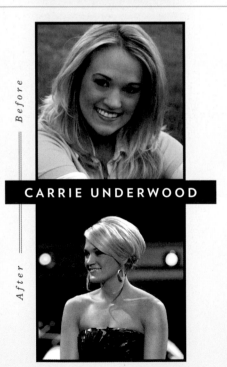

Before

CARRIE UNDERWOOD

After

Before

KELLIE PICKLER

After

FAUX HAWKS

1. SANJAYA MALAKAR
2. SIOBHAN MAGNUS
3. NADIA TURNER

①

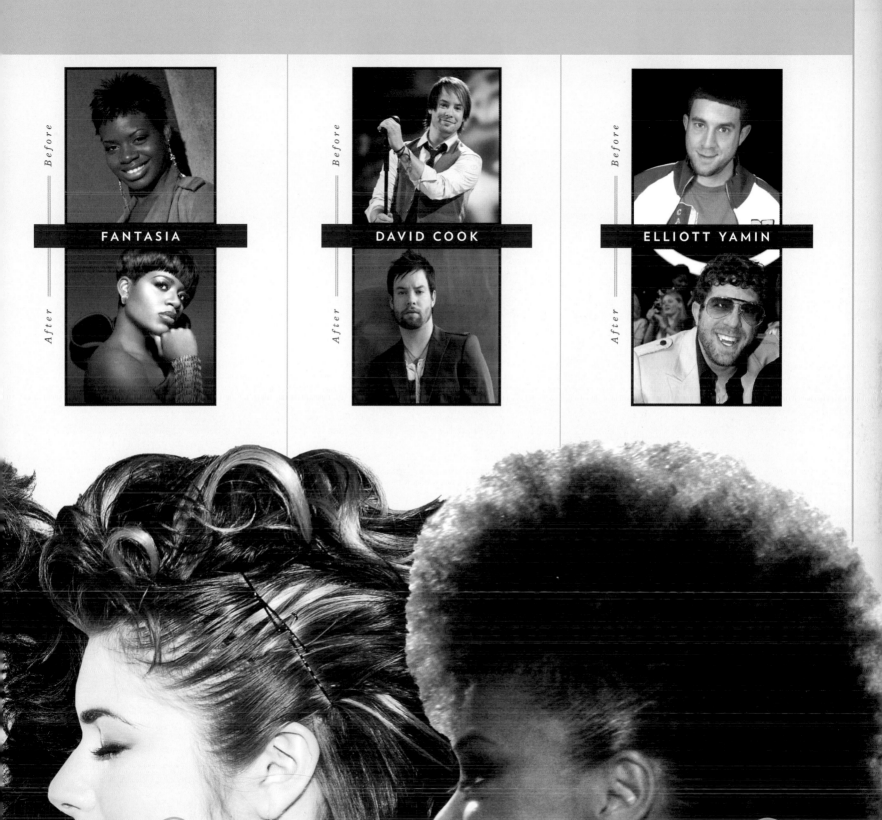

Before

FANTASIA

After

Before

DAVID COOK

After

Before

ELLIOTT YAMIN

After

②

③

IDOL HEARTTHROBS

ACE YOUNG: With his long, flowing locks, those chocolate-brown eyes, and a radiant smile, season five's Ace Young had the ladies in the *Idol* studio swooning on first sight— and his voice wasn't bad, either.

CHRIS RICHARDSON: Season six's Justin Timberlake look- and sound-alike was Virginia's own Chris Richardson, who opted for more contemporary fare when it came to his *Idol* performances. His look, on the other hand, was a complete throwback.

MICHAEL JOHNS: Australian import and former tennis player, Michael Johns was one of four season seven finalists to score high on the sexy scale—and with an enchanting accent to boot!

JASON CASTRO: His dreadlocks may have thrown some season seven viewers for a loop, but there was no denying Jason Castro's piercing blue eyes, silky-smooth skin, and sweet—and sometimes spacey—stare.

DAVID ARCHULETA: He defined adorable in season seven, what with those irresistible dimples and "aw shucks" grin, but it was David Archuleta's angelic voice that sent millions of teenage hearts aflutter.

DAVID COOK: When season seven began, David Cook was a diamond in the rough. By show's end, he emerged not only as a victor but a bona fide rock star, complete with piercing gaze and just the right amount of rolled-out-of-bed stubble.

MATT GIRAUD: When it comes to the ladies, season eight's piano man teased on top ten week with a sexy version of Marvin Gaye's "Let's Get It On."

ADAM LAMBERT: Female fandom hit a fever pitch when season eight's Adam Lambert came into the picture and delivered dramatic, nuanced performances the likes of which *Idol* viewers had never seen or heard. Part Elvis, part Mick Jagger, with a hint of Steven Tyler and a whole lot of swagger, he redefined the *Idol* archetype with the wave of a fingerless-gloved hand.

KRIS ALLEN: The season eight winner didn't scream heartthrob when he first faced the judges, and even well into the competition, Kris Allen readily admitted feeling awkward when *Idol* photographers would ask for his "sexy face," but there's no denying this doe-eyed cutie pie.

TIM URBAN: His ear-to-ear smile and flop-top hair were all the rage during season nine, but beyond the dashing good looks, Tim Urban was a consummate charmer. It's no wonder he made it to seventh place.

AARON KELLY: Season nine's youngest finalist was a hopeful of few words, but when Aaron Kelly spoke, people listened. Was it the mesmerizing baby blue eyes or his soft delivery and gentlemanly mannerisms?

CASEY JAMES: Tall, rugged, blond, blue-eyed, and undeniably handsome, Casey James had the cougars of America going gaga for most of season nine. Was Casey's top four rendition of "Mrs. Robinson" his way of showing appreciation for a loyal female fan base? If so, well-played, cowboy.

AMERICAN IDOL STYLE

11

CHAPTER 11: **SEASON SIX**

11

IN WHAT WAS UNDOUBTEDLY one of *Idol*'s most eclectic seasons, the class of 2007 seemed to throw caution to the wind in its bid to expand the show's song catalog. But in the end, it came down to pop star–ready potential, which then-seventeen-year-old Jordin Sparks had in spades, versus quirkiness in the form of a beat boxer with boundless talent, Blake Lewis.

Jordin came to the competition a quiet but confident daughter of a football star—poised and pretty, but without all that unnecessary flash. And she impressed big time. Between ballads like Martina McBride's "Broken Wing" and The Bee Gees' classic "To Love Somebody" and up-tempo numbers like Gloria Estefan's "Rhythm Is Gonna Get You" and Pat Benatar's "Heartbreaker," there wasn't a genre she couldn't handle, as demonstrated time and time again.

Of course, she wasn't the only one fighting for that one top spot. In third place, but long considered a front-runner, was Melinda Doolittle, a little Southern soul sister who had the voice of an angel. Right behind her: LaKisha Jones, a belter with some serious conviction. As for the guys, Justin Timberlake sound- and look-alike Chris Richardson had the girls' votes, while Sanjaya . . . The jury's still out on that one, but it all made for one heck of an entertaining showdown.

Then there was Blake. As one of *Idol*'s most eccentric graduates, he influenced the competition immeasur-

ably, prompting the producers to consider allowing instruments (which they did the following year), expanding the contestants' view of an *Idol*-appropriate song library with unexpected choices, and taking liberties with melody and structure the likes of which had never been tried before. Look no further than his take on The Zombies' "Time of the Season" or his introduction of reggae rockers 311 to the *Idol* audience, not to mention his most memorable mash up, Bon Jovi's "You Give Love a Bad Name."

Season six also introduced the world to what would become *Idol* institutions: Idol Gives Back, the massive charity effort that has raised hundreds of millions of dollars to combat world poverty, provide relief in disaster areas, and aid in various health crises. The first of three star-studded shows began during season six and raised more than $70 million. And, to a far lesser extent, Crying Girl, then-thirteen-year-old Ashley Ferl, who had the first of many teary breakdowns after Sanjaya Malakar performed The Kinks' "You Really Got Me."

In the end, it was *Idol* that had gotten a really good hold of America, as seasoned artists like Jennifer Lopez, Gwen Stefani, and Tony Bennett lined up for a chance to be mentors and, even more, offered their services for the finale, among them Green Day and Bette Midler! My, how far the show had come . . .

CLASS *of* 07

SEASON 6 YEARBOOK

"You're a young Tina Turner and vocally, you're in a different league than everyone else." —Simon Cowell

MELINDA DOOLITTLE

"Backup Singer"

STEPHANIE EDWARDS

"Singer"

GINA GLOCKSEN

"Dental Assistant"

LAKISHA JONES

"Bank Teller"

SEASON 6
RUNNER-UP
2007

BLAKE LEWIS

"Musician"

SANJAYA MALAKAR

"Student"

"You are a contemporary rebel in this competition." —Randy Jackson

"you have a likeability about you." —Simon Cowell

CHRIS RICHARDSON

"Kitchen Supervisor"

BRANDON ROGERS

"Backup Singer"

HALEY SCARNATO

"Former Wedding Singer"

CHRIS SLIGH

"Musician"

SEASON 6
WINNER!
2007

JORDIN SPARKS

"Student"

PHIL STACEY

"Navy"

Looking back with the season six champ

You were 17 during Idol, how did your age factor into the competition?

Jordin Sparks: It was both an advantage and a disadvantage. On one hand, it was nice being told I had "such a huge voice for someone so young," but the judges also told younger contestants they weren't ready. In the back of my mind, I was always waiting for them to say that to me. Thankfully, they never did. Sanjaya was the only person close to my age in the top 12, everyone else was at least four years older, but I relate to people older than me. My mom always said I was "mature for my age," and even Randy said, "You have an old soul." And I agree.

Take us back to the night the Top 3 was announced, what was going through your mind?

JS: My first thought was, "I hope Lakisha is okay!" It was always tough when someone left because we all got extremely close. I never looked at the other contestants as competition because they were my friends. I always wanted to top myself and saw myself from the week before as the person to beat. I don't know if I felt I could win at that point, honestly. I thought it was going to be Blake and Melinda in the final two all along. But the contest seemed to shift because there were now three completely different singers to vote for.

When it came down to you and Blake and victory was in sight, did you formulate a strategy?

JS: I was always thinking about our how our fan bases developed over the season, and I'd try to figure out who had the biggest advantage. It was pretty even in my eyes. My only strategy was trying to get through the week before the finale. The top 2 have it the hardest because, besides our songs, the duets and all the press we had to do, we also had to learn the group performances! We were ready to collapse!

What surprised you most about the American Idol experience?

JS: I didn't realize how big of a phenomenon it was until I was on the inside. We worked our butts off doing interviews, photo shoots, questionnaires, picking our outfits, filming Ford commercials, the mentor shoots, choosing our songs, cutting our songs down and trying to find time to sleep. It was insane but it definitely prepared me for the future!

What was your favorite moment of season 6?

JS: Sheesh, there were a ton. I loved Inspirational Songs week and Idol Gives Back. As stressful as that was, it was nice to give and be a part of it. And winning was one of my favorite moments, too! [Laughs]

WINNER'S CIRCLE

JORDIN SPARKS

* **HOMETOWN:** Glendale, Arizona

* **AUDITION SONG:** "Because You Loved Me" by Celine Dion

* **WORDS TO LIVE BY:** *"She has a star quality because of her smile and you see the glitter, the shine in her eyes. She has an inner light which is very important."* —Diana Ross

* **LIFE AFTER IDOL:** At seventeen years old, Jordin Sparks became the youngest *Idol* winner ever when she beat Blake Lewis in the season six finale. And after the summer of 2007 Idol tour, the teen with the fierce pipes wasted no time releasing her platinum-selling self-titled debut. The album yielded no less than four hits in the top twenty of music charts, including "Tattoo" and "No Air," her duet with Chris Brown, which quickly turned into a quan-

tifiable radio smash. The album was a winner all around, earning her two MTV Video Music Awards nominations, an American Music Awards nod in 2008, and a Grammy nomination.

Jordin's second studio effort, *Battlefield,* was released in 2009 and debuted at number seven, while the title track cracked the top ten of the *Billboard* Hot 100 and sold more than a million copies. She scored her first number one hit with "S.O.S. (Let the Music Play)," which topped the *Billboard* Hot Dance Club Play chart in 2009. Jordin opened up for megastar Alicia Keys on her As I Am tour and co-headlined a tour with Jesse McCartney.

Expanding her scope outside of music, Jordin also partnered with Wet Seal to design her own clothing line, Sparks. On the small screen, America's newest sweetheart guest starred on Disney's *The Suite Life on Deck* and Nickelodeon's *Big Time Rush.* In 2010, she got top billing in the Broadway smash *In the Heights,* to rave reviews.

BLAKE LEWIS

* **HOMETOWN:** Bothell, Washington

* **AUDITION SONG:** "Crazy" by Seal

* **WORDS TO LIVE BY:** *"I will give you the award for most original version of a song ever on* American Idol. *You took a leap of faith and you won."* —Randy

* **LIFE AFTER IDOL:** Blake Lewis made it all the way to second place by turning the *Idol* formula on its head, so it was no surprise that his post-show album would feature his acute appreciation of pop coupled with eccentric dance styles and beats that would make any club kid proud.

His 2007 Arista Records debut *A.D.D. (Audio Day Dream)* peaked at number ten on the *Billboard* 200 chart, eventually selling more than 300,000 copies. After parting ways with the Sony-owned label in 2008, he signed with respected dance-hip-hop label Tommy Boy Records and released his sophomore effort, *Heartbreak on Vinyl,* in October 2009. Its first single, "Sad Song," also reached the top ten of *Billboard's* Dance Radio

Airplay chart while the album made the *Billboard* 200, the Independent Albums chart, and the Billboard Dance/Electronic Albums chart. In other words, it was a DIY hit. Bringing the dance-floor fun to the people, Blake travels extensively all over America and Europe performing for adoring and loyal fans that are still voting, only now with their hard-earned dollars.

Also thanks to *Idol,* Blake added heartthrob to his résumé when he made several lists of sexiest contestants ever. AOL.com ranked him number twenty-one on its countdown of sexiest single men and *People* magazine named him one of the hottest bachelors of 2007.

MELINDA DOOLITTLE

* **HOMETOWN:** Brentwood, Tennessee

* **AUDITION SONG:** "For Once in My Life" by Stevie Wonder

* **WORDS TO LIVE BY:** *"You are very, very good. You remind me of a young Gladys Knight."* —Simon

* **LIFE AFTER IDOL:** Any preconceived notions about Melinda Doolittle's petite frame or soft demeanor went out the window the minute *Idol* viewers heard that huge voice. No wonder she was the shining star of the American Idols Live! Tour, receiving rave reviews for her standout performances, like when the *New York Times* called her "a phenomenally gifted, stylistically adroit Gladys Knight–Tina Turner hybrid."

To wit, shortly after she was eliminated in third

place, Simon Cowell told *Good Morning America* he felt Melinda was the rightful season six winner. And while history could not be rewritten, she put her pipes to good use singing at the White House and NBA Finals in 2007, the same year she released her first digital single, "My Funny Valentine."

In 2009, Melinda signed to independent label Hi-Fi Recordings and released her debut album, *Coming Back to You*, which had more than respectable sales and features a broad array of covers, from classic blues songs to contemporary fare.

Outside of music, her Web series, *Moments with Melinda*, gave fans a chance to connect directly with their favorite Idol, and Melinda went on to write a piece included in *Chicken Soup for the American Idol Soul.* She has also been heavily involved in the charity Malaria No More and even visited Africa with First Lady Laura Bush to distribute life-changing supplies and raise awareness.

LAKISHA JONES

* **HOMETOWN:** Fort Meade, Maryland
* **AUDITION SONG:** "Think" by Aretha Franklin

* **WORDS TO LIVE BY:** *"You're a beautiful performer. You're a beautiful girl and your heart comes through when you sing, which is the most important thing you can possess as an artist."* —Paula

* **LIFE AFTER *IDOL*:** Although this powerhouse vocalist didn't make it to the finale, LaKisha Jones's fans gave her a true hero's homecoming following her fourth-place elimination. Sure she may not have won *Idol*, but she won the heart of the city of her birth, Flint, Michigan, where she was awarded a brand-new Buick LaCrosse, a $6,000 check, and the honor of "LaKisha Jones Day" by Michigan's governor. In Dallas, Texas, where she had lived for six years, Houston Mayor Bill White also declared a day in her honor.

In 2008, LaKisha joined the cast of the Broadway musical *The Color Purple* as the church soloist, and stood in for Chaka Khan as Sofia during matinees. The same year, she was also featured as a vocal coach and mentor on MTV's *Legally Blonde: The Search for Elle Woods*. As for her own singing career, she released her debut album, *So Glad I'm Me*, in May 2009, performing the single, "Just as I Am," a few months earlier on *American Idol Extra*.

CHRIS RICHARDSON

* **HOMETOWN:** Chesapeake, Virginia
* **AUDITION SONG:** "A Song for You" by Leon Russell/Donny Hathaway

* **WORDS TO LIVE BY:** *"Chris is in it to win it tonight, dogg! I even think that was hotter than the original."* —Randy

* **LIFE AFTER *IDOL*:** On the show, Chris Richardson remained one of the most popular members of the top ten to travel on the American Idols Live! Tour. Following the three-month-long trek, he went on to release his debut single, "All Alone" in 2008, followed by a ten-city outing sponsored by Dreyers.

Chris penned the track "What'cha Got 2 Lose?" for buddy Blake Lewis's album, *A.D.D.*, and released a bonus track on iTunes titled, "Human." He also wrote songs for Jordin Sparks and Phil Stacey. In 2008, he performed at Jason Mraz's Music, Magic, and Makepeace tour, dazzling crowds with the scatlike duet "Geek in the Pink." In 2009, he walked the red carpet at the season nine *Idol* finale and bid Simon Cowell one final good-bye during his tribute performance.

PHIL STACEY

✳ **HOMETOWN:** Jacksonville, Florida

✳ **AUDITION SONG:** "My Girl" by The Temptations

✳ **WORDS TO LIVE BY:** *"You're reminiscent of a young Frank Sinatra."* —Paula

✳ **LIFE AFTER *IDOL*:** After completing his stint on the Live! tour and rejoining his wife and children in Florida, Phil Stacey took Randy's advice and tried his luck at country music. He signed with Lyric Street Records in 2007 and released his debut single, "If You Didn't Love Me," in 2008. It peaked at number twenty-eight on the *Billboard* Hot Country Songs chart and was written by Rascal Flatts front man Gary LeVox. In 2009, Phil signed with Christian label Reunion Records and released his full-length debut, *Into the Light*, in August 2009.

SANJAYA MALAKAR

✳ **HOMETOWN:** Federal Way, Washington

✳ **AUDITION SONG:** "Signed, Sealed, Delivered, I'm Yours" by Stevie Wonder

✳ **WORDS TO LIVE BY:** *"To me, Sanjaya is love."* —Diana Ross

✳ **LIFE AFTER *IDOL*:** Sanjaya's super-successful *Idol* run was only the beginning of his fandamonium. Following the Live! tour, he met President

George W. Bush at the White House Correspondents' Dinner, where he was an invited guest of *People* magazine. Subsequent to the appearance, his face was plastered across the pages of every magazine imaginable—he was even featured in *Time*'s prestigious 100 Most Influential People of the Year.

It goes without saying, but as a pop-culture icon, few have had the staying power of Sanjaya, who nabbed the honor of Best Reality Star at the 2007 Teen Choice Awards. Even the popularity of his *Idol* performances didn't wane when the red light turned off. His performance of No Doubt's "Bathwater" remains among the highest ranked TV moments on AOL.

Like most *Idol* alums, he also made the television rounds, appearing on *The Tonight Show*, *Good Morning America*, *Live with Regis and Kelly*, and *The Ellen DeGeneres Show*, among many others. In 2009, he added author to his résumé when he penned an autobiography, *Dancing to the Music in My Head: Memoirs of the People's Idol*. Later that year, he returned

to his reality TV roots in the second season of *I'm a Celebrity . . . Get Me Outta Here!* He is currently attending Cornish College of the Arts with his sister and fellow former *Idol* hopeful Shyamali Malakar.

HALEY SCARNATO

✳ **HOMETOWN:** San Antonio, Texas

✳ **AUDITION SONG:** "I Can't Make You Love Me" by Bonnie Raitt

✳ **WORDS TO LIVE BY:** *"Leaps and bounds better than last week. More of you having fun and we get to see your personality, which is good."* —Paula

✳ **LIFE AFTER *IDOL*:** While this Idol may have gained more notoriety for her looks than her voice, the Texan beauty held her own alongside her season six cast mates during the Live! tour. Haley Scarnato has gone one to perform the national anthem at major games like the 2007 NBA semifinals between the San Antonio Spurs and Dallas Mavericks, and again for game two of the same matchup in 2009. The studio versions of recording artist Haley's *Idol* performances are available on iTunes, but she has yet to release a proper first album.

GINA GLOCKSEN

* **HOMETOWN:** Naperville, Illinois

* **AUDITION SONG:** "Black Velvet" by Alannah Myles

* **WORDS TO LIVE BY:** *"It's all about knowing who you are, choosing the right song. The transformation from three to four weeks ago to tonight is literally chalk and cheese. It was the best performance of the night, that's how good it was."* —Simon

* **LIFE AFTER *IDOL*:** If you're going out on *Idol*, Charlie Chaplin's "Smile" is just about the most optimistic swan song one could have. Gina Glocksen made the TV rounds from there, performing "Home" on *Ellen* and appearing on *Live with Regis and Kelly* and Nickelodeon's ME:TV, then rejoining her season six cast mates for the 2007 summer tour. During a stop in Illinois, Gina's longtime boyfriend, Joe, surprised her with a marriage proposal onstage. (Fellow season sixers Jordin Sparks and Haley Scarnato were bridesmaids at her 2009 wedding.) The following year, Gina cohosted *American Idol Extra* with season four alum Constantine Maroulis, and it was there that she premiered her single "When It Rains." Clearly, it's all about keeping things in the *Idol* family.

CHRIS SLIGH

* **HOMETOWN:** Greenville, South Carolina

* **AUDITION SONG:** "Kiss from a Rose" by Seal

* **WORDS TO LIVE BY:** *"This shows that you've got that big voice. You've got skills, too, so always rely on that and remember that."* —Randy

* **LIFE AFTER *IDOL*:** Chris Sligh's strong vocals and lovable personality made him a judge's favorite from the start. Although this Southern sweetie managed to crack the top ten, he was sent home that week, following an upbeat performance of The Police classic "Every Little Thing She Does Is Magic." Following the Live! tour, he signed a deal with Atlanta-based indie label Brash Music and released his first album, *Running Back to You,* in 2008. His first single, "Empty Me," hit number six on the *Billboard* Hot Christian Songs chart and was featured on *Billboard* magazine's Top Heatseekers chart. The critically acclaimed LP gained popularity on Christian radio and prompted a thirty-two-city tour and more than 115 performances. The same year, he toured with NewSong on its Christmas Celebration tour, hitting eighteen cities across the country.

In 2009, Sligh wrote the hit "Here Comes Goodbye" for country music superstars Rascal Flatts. The song peaked at number one and spent twelve weeks on the *Billboard* Hot Country chart. The same year, he released his Christmas album on iTunes and signed with the Christian arm of a major label, Word Records. Following his second Back to School tour, he began work on his next album, *Anatomy of Broken*. Also on his 2010 to-do list: fatherhood—Sligh's wife gave birth to a baby girl in October of that year.

STEPHANIE EDWARDS

* **HOMETOWN:** Savannah, Georgia

* **AUDITION SONG:** Unaired

* **WORDS TO LIVE BY:** *"You sang your face off. You proved you're supposed to be up there."* —Randy

* **LIFE AFTER *IDOL*:** Stephanie Edwards's performance of "Sweet Thing" was called "darn near flawless" by the judges, and her rendition of Beyoncé's "Crazy in Love" prompted Randy to declare that she "sang her face off." Still, this Southern soul sister was the second contestant to go home on season six. Following her elimination in British Invasion Week, the Georgia peach recorded a single, "On Our Way," for the Leukemia & Lymphoma Society's Light the Night Walk. She released a second single, "Here I Am," in 2008 and currently performs in *Southern Nights*, a local review show in Savannah, singing covers and classics for her hometown fans.

BRANDON ROGERS

* **HOMETOWN:** North Hollywood, California

* **AUDITION SONG:** "Always on My Mind" by Elvis Presley

* **WORDS TO LIVE BY:** *"I felt you in my heart and that's how I can tell, beautiful."* —Olivia Newton-John

* **LIFE AFTER *IDOL*:** He was everybody's pal on season six, and long after his top twelve showing, this SoCal local and all-around nice guy remains an ambassador of sorts for Idols past and present. Of course, it was Brandon Rogers's singing that prompted Simon to call him the best of that bunch, even if his first week performance of "You Can't Hurry Love" sent him packing. Already an accomplished backup singer before *Idol*, Brandon continued pursuing his music after the show. He also gave acting a try, appearing on FOX's hit series *Bones* in 2008. The same year, he headlined a live show in Branson, Missouri, called *America's Favorite Finalists* alongside fellow *Idol* alums.

Greatest Hits

A BROKEN WING

JORDIN SPARKS

APRIL 17, 2007

The season six champ's rendition of superstar mentor Martina McBride's "A Broken Wing" soared during Country Week and was so fantastic she repeated it on her triumphant finale night. It prompted Simon to correctly predict she would win the show, and Paula noted, "You have a beautiful way of telling a story. It was gorgeous." Sparks's appearance was equally stunning; she was radiant in a red gown and long flowing tresses.

YOU GIVE LOVE A BAD NAME

BLAKE LEWIS

MAY 1, 2007

Blake's brave, beat-boxing adaptation of Bon Jovi's classic "You Give Love a Bad Name" was a risk worth taking. The judges absolutely loved his dramatic changes and unique delivery. Randy called it "the most original version of a song ever on *American Idol*," and said, "you took a leap of faith and you won." The audience agreed and showed their support with a standing ovation while Paula gave a shout-out to Simon's mother whom she saw "rockin' out to it."

TROUBLE IS A WOMAN

MELINDA DOOLITTLE

APRIL 17, 2007

Melinda's sassy choice of "Trouble Is a Woman" on the country-themed night proved she had range and attitude, to boot. She wowed judges with a new sexy, straight 'do and animated performance. Randy crowned her the show's resident pro and Paula commented, "Once again, a girl who knows how to pick the right song, sing her heart out, and perform like there's no tomorrow."

THIS AIN'T A LOVE SONG

LAKISHA JONES

MAY 1, 2007

Lakisha's powerful pipes were on full display when she belted Bon Jovi's "This Ain't a Love Song" in week eight, while her sexy style choice for the night—straight hair, and a black, curve-hugging ensemble—wowed the judges on every level. In fact, LaKisha's performance was so amazing it seemed to melt even Simon's icy heart, prompting him to peck her on the lips after exclaiming, "I could kiss you after that. You're so good." Paula saw dollar signs in the soul singer's future, saying, "That low tone in your voice is money in your pocket."

WHERE THE BLACKTOP ENDS

PHIL STACEY

APRIL 17, 2007

Phil Stacey was onto something when he chose Keith Urban's "Where the Blacktop Ends" on the country-themed night. He delivered an energetic, crowd-pleasing performance, dancing through the audience while impressing the judges with spot-on vocals—no small feat! Paula praised his performance from beginning to end, and Randy declared, "As an established music producer, I have to say you could have a real career in country music, man."

The UNDER 18 CLUB

FRESH-FACED, FEARLESS YOUNGSTERS WHO SWAPPED SCHOOLBOOKS FOR SONGBOOKS AND HEADED TO HOLLYWOOD FOR THE CHANCE OF A LIFETIME, ALL BEFORE THEY HIT THE BIG ONE-EIGHT.

JORDIN SPARKS
SEVENTEEN

PARIS BENNETT
SEVENTEEN

JASMINE TRIAS
SEVENTEEN

SANJAYA MALAKAR
SEVENTEEN

JOHN STEVENS
SIXTEEN

DAVID ARCHULETA
SIXTEEN

LEAH LABELLE
SEVENTEEN

ALLISON IRAHETA
SIXTEEN

DIANA DeGARMO
SIXTEEN

JASMINE MURRAY
SIXTEEN

MIKALAH GORDON
SEVENTEEN

AARON KELLY
SEVENTEEN

KEVIN COVAIS
SIXTEEN

KATIE STEVENS
SEVENTEEN

American Idol

SEASON 6

BACKSTAGE PASS

RYAN SEACREST 101

When Ryan Seacrest took center stage for *American Idol*'s premiere in 2002, he had only an inkling of what he was signing up for: to help launch new talent into super-stardom. What Ryan couldn't predict, however, was that he too would be catapulted to new heights in show business and become one of the most powerful players in entertainment.

The Atlanta native, who had worked in radio since he was a teenager, moved to Los Angeles in 1993 and spent nearly a decade raising his Hollywood profile. Small-time hosting gigs (*Radical Outdoor Challenge* on ESPN, *Saturday Night at the Movies* on NBC, a reality show called *Ultimate Revenge*, and the kids show *Gladiators 2000*) were his entrée to television, but Ryan's big break arrived when he was asked to host a new singing competition on FOX. Like its British predecessor, *Pop Idol*, *American Idol* initially featured a second host, comedian Brian Dunkleman, but there was no doubt that Seacrest was a star, and after season one brought in 26 million viewers, he returned as the sole host for the show's second year.

Guiding audiences from auditions through Hollywood week, the top twenty-four (or thirty-six, as in season eight) to the top twelve (or thirteen—season eight again) to the final two, Ryan's effervescent personality and constant back-and-forth bickering with Simon Cowell gave viewers a hero to rally behind and the contestants a shoulder to lean on—and made his signature sign-off, "Seacrest Out," a pop culture footnote and national punch line.

In 2004, Ryan took the reins of *American Top 40*, the weekly radio countdown show created by iconic host, and Ryan's own Idol, Casey Kasem. Not long after, he moved over to L.A.'s popular KIIS FM morning show, and *On Air with Ryan Seacrest* was born. As host and executive producer of the show, *On Air* has achieved great success and is broadcast on more than 150 U.S. radio stations as well as international affiliates.

Ryan joined his other idol, Dick Clark, in 2005 for the annual *Dick Clark's New Year's Rockin' Eve* special and did such a good job handling hosting duties for the ailing Clark—with much-appreciated sensitivity—that he was asked to continue hosting and coproducing the show, adding his name to the title. In 2006, Ryan signed a multiyear, multimillion-dollar deal with the E! Network, where he would host their daily entertainment news show, produce original programming, and serve as the network's red carpet correspondent. The same year, he won an Emmy Award for his cohosting duties on Walt Disney World's Christmas Day Parade with Regis Philbin and Kelly Ripa. Ryan went on to host the *Primetime Emmy Awards* in 2007 and 2008.

His production company, Ryan Seacrest Productions, or RSP, has seen massive success as well, thanks to the hit reality show *Keeping Up with the Kardashians*, which spawned a spin-off series, *Kourtney & Khloe Take Miami* in 2009. Ryan also produced original programming for MTV, including the short-lived show *Bromance* starring Brody Jenner, and was the executive producer on *Jamie Oliver's Food Revolution*, broadcast on ABC in 2010. The year 2009 proved to be another landmark moment for Ryan, when he inked a record-breaking deal with CKX, making him the highest-paid reality host ever.

OFF-SCRIPT SEACREST

AT LEAST ONCE A SEASON, HOST RYAN SEACREST FANCIES HIMSELF A COMEDIAN. HERE, A COLLECTION OF RYAN'S KOOKIER MOMENTS AND OFF-THE-PROMPTER MUSINGS.

Splitting hosting duties on season one, Ryan Seacrest and Brian Dunkleman were still adjusting to *American Idol*'s instant popularity. "It's the FOX show that everybody's talking about," said Ryan before introducing the top six and himself: *"I'm Ryan Seacrest, and I'm asking for more money."*

Dollar signs were still on Ryan's mind in season two. Cutting to a break after Josh Gracin performed "Piano Man" on Billy Joel Week, Ryan joked: *"I hate to break the flow, but without these commercials, none of us would get paid and daddy needs new highlights."*

By season four, Ryan was poking fun at himself regularly, like when he opened up the show with this zinger: *"New singers, same overly made-up host."* More often, however, it was Simon on the receiving end of Ryan's cracks, like when the host introduced a 1990s theme to the top ten by cracking, *"We're celebrating the decade when Simon bought his first T-shirt and he's still wearing it tonight, ladies and gentlemen."*

Here was a season five moment for the history book: In sympathizing with Mandisa, who had to wear painfully high heels for her top twelve performance of Stevie Wonder's "Don't You Worry 'bout a Thing," Ryan offered her a foot massage then proceeded to remove her shoes on live television. *"You have nice moisturized ankles here,"* he said, before handing a stilleto to Simon.

Taylor Hicks's Country Week performance of John Denver's "Country Roads, Take Me Home" didn't exactly impress the judges, or one in particular who called it "safe, boring and lazy." Ryan's retort? *"Safe boring and lazy ... Simon's love life ladies and gentlemen!"*

In another kooky season five moment, Ryan joined Taylor Hicks on the floor and on their backs while reading the top four hopeful's phone numbers.

It was the first top twelve show of season seven, and while the contestants had changed, some things remained the same. To illustrate, Ryan told Carly Smithson, *"We've got this new set, but we still have the most uncomfortable stools in television history."*

Ryan didn't miss a beat with his reaction to Nick Mitchell's alter ego Norman Gentle in the semifinals. The zany rendition of "And I Am Telling You I'm Not Going," which found the top twenty-four contender writhing on the floor, prompted Ryan to muse, *"That is the first time that a contestant has gone to second base with our logo."*

Ryan's most outlandish act on season nine was a work of waltz, not words. During Tim Urban's Elvis Week performance of "I Can't Help Falling in Love," he got cornered behind the judges' table and rather than dashing across the studio, Ryan opted for an off-camera dance with a random but burly audience member.

RYAN'S

Hair Color

WHEEL

2002
2003
2004
2005
2006
2007
2008
2009
2010

2002 – FROSTY THE SEACREST

Ryan Seacrest was *Idol* gold from the start! Look no further than his season one–era frosted blond tips for proof. Even more piercing? The hand-twisted spikes atop his head. Can't you just smell the gel?

2003 – AMBER WAVES

In year two, Ryan settled into his role as host of America's number one show, and so did his hair, which went from platinum shades of gray to a strawberry blond wave symbolic of his ability to always go with the flow.

2004 – THE BUTTERFLY *or* THE SURFRIDER

Continuing to relax the tint and intensity of his cut, Ryan put a little swing in his hairstyle step for season three, in the form of a dip and a curl. The blond highlights? Replaced by more subtle low lights.

2005 – BUZZWORTHY

Ryan kept his brown 'do buzzed for much of year four, in stark contrast to the guy he shared the stage with all season long: proud longhair Bo Bice.

2006 – STUBBLED UPON

Matching facial hair to head, Ryan sported a five o'clock shadow on and off during season five.

2007 – FAUX FAUX HAWK

Proving he's just as willing as Paula in the poke-fun-at-yourself department, Ryan rocked a Sanjaya-style wig one time in season six.

2008 – THE ELVIS

Ryan returned to his Southern roots—and finally, his natural hair color—for season seven, sporting a modern-day version of the Elvis Presley.

2009 – TCB

Ryan's reputation as a media mogul hit critical mass in his eighth year as host, and with that pop culture responsibility came a haircut that also aimed to show he meant business.

2010 – THE SPRINGBOARD

With the slightest hint of *Jersey Shore* influence, Ryan—and his hair—reached for the stars in season nine.

> *People bring up my hair quite a bit. It's strategically tousled. The flatiron is key.*
>
> – RYAN SEACREST

13

IT WAS THE SEASON THAT marked the epic battle of the Davids, pinning twenty-eight-year-old rocker David Cook against seventeen-year-old cutie crooner David Archuleta. The competition was intense from the get-go. Cook, an accidental auditioner who had basically shown up with his brother at the St. Louis tryouts and decided on a whim to give it a shot, took music very seriously. Ditto for Archie, who had competed on *Star Search 3* and even amazed *Idol*'s season one crew during a tour stop in 2002 when he was all of twelve years old—the performance, a spot-on rendition of *Dreamgirls*' "And I Am Telling You I'm Not Going," lives on in YouTube popularity. As the weeks went on, Cook upped his game, delivering nuanced performances that often twisted the original melodies in ways no one could have imagined. It got the judges' attention, but not necessarily their respect—at least not Simon's.

And who could blame him? Season seven boasted some of the strongest talent *Idol* had ever seen. Third-placer Syesha Mercado could sing circles around even the most seasoned stage star; Jason Castro perfected the art of less is more with stripped-down, quiet performances that brought out his sensitivity, silky voice, and those icy blue eyes. The pair of Carly Smithson and Michael Johns, in addition to Cook, provided a recipe for rock 'n' roll that the show had rarely experienced. You could say the same of Brooke White, who famously started, stopped, and restarted two of her performances, moves that didn't exactly impress the judges, no matter how smooth. Thankfully, her singing and playing skills did.

"Playing" is the key word as season seven was the first to allow contestants their own instrumental accompaniment. This meant that, even though it was only ninety seconds of performance time, David Cook could at least attempt to rock his Les Paul, which was adorned with the initials of his brother Adam, who was battling brain cancer. Even season four's Bo Bice got to enjoy this new perk when he returned to the show and was able to play his own guitar on center stage for the very first time.

Indeed, in its seventh year, *Idol* boasted so many successful alums that it was getting hard to keep count; but where the show could involve past winners it did, not the least of which included that year's Idol Gives Back initiatives along with the exit song, a cover of Kenny Loggins's "Celebrate Me Home," recorded by season two winner Ruben Studdard.

By the time the finale came around, the results were nearly impossible to predict as both Davids enjoyed impassioned fan bases, the faith of label veteran Clive Davis, and the support of Paula Abdul, who barely sat once during the hour-long performance round. Then there was Simon, who declared that Archie delivered a "knockout" with his final three performances, only to apologize to Cook the following night for not giving him proper due. In the end, Simon said he didn't care who would win as both deserved to be in the finals. Said Randy, "I'm so happy it's the two of you standing there." But in the end, it came down to one. And rather than his usual cool-as-a-cucumber vibe (even more so after a high blood pressure reading sent him to the hospital midseason), Cook finally let it all out in a glorious, emotional finish to an unforgettable run.

CLASS *of*

08

SEASON 7 YEARBOOK

"David, you can sing the phone book and we'd fall in love with that." —Paula Abdul

"He's got the right material, he's got right attitude, he's got the right voice he'll do great, no doubt about it." —Neil Diamond

SEASON 7
RUNNER-UP
2008

SEASON 7
WINNER!
2008

DAVID ARCHULETA
"High School Student"

JASON CASTRO
"College Student"

DAVID COOK
"Bartender-Musician"

KRISTY LEE COOK
"Horse Trainer"

CHIKEZIE EZE
"TSA Officer at LAX"

DAVID HERNANDEZ
"Student-Waiter"

"Your vocals sound really good... I'm very proud of you." —Paula Abdul

"You're a force to be reckoned with . . .
There's such a beautiful range in your voice."
—Paula Abdul

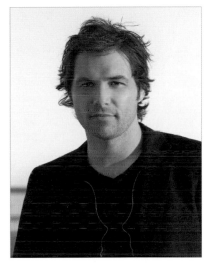

MICHAEL JOHNS

"Singer"

RAMIELE MALUBAY

"Sushi Restaurant Employee"

SYESHA MERCADO

"Student-Actress"

AMANDA OVERMYER

"Nurse"

CARLY SMITHSON

"Singer-Bartender-Waitress-
Tattoo Shop Owner"

BROOKE WHITE

"Nanny"

Looking back with the season seven champ

From the beginning, you had an air of confidence about you. Where did that come from?

David Cook: I was an unfinished product, a little rough around the edges, but I knew what I wanted to do and where my voice sat on the musical spectrum. Within the show parameters, the confidence came from finally getting a good review that third week after performing "Hello." I thought there was no way I would make the top twelve and I had joked about doing Lionel Richie as a power ballad, thinking if I'm going out, what a way to do it! And they loved it. After that, I just followed my gut, and if a song didn't grab me in the first twenty seconds, I chose something else.

What was special about season seven?

DC: We just all got along. I hear stories of other seasons not getting along as much and it's weird to me. I think we realized we're not competing against each other as much as it's played up. We're all different singers and people and can certainly coexist, so we just had fun with it. I stood side stage and cheered everybody on. There was a lot of talent in my season.

How did the whole David vs. David thing sit with you?

DC: Good marketing, I suppose. At that point, I just wanted to get there—if it was me versus whoever. But I don't know if there's anyone I would've gone against where I might have felt like "I got this." I was confident in my abilities, but I still contend that if it was a singing competition, there's no way I would have won. I look at Syesha or Archie or Carly or Michael who all had incredible voices and I'm still at a loss for what exactly put me over the top, but I'll take it.

Was there a moment during the finale when you just took it all in or was the whole night just a blur?

DC: There really wasn't. I took it all in at the season eight finale. [Laughs] I still don't remember some of it. At that point, Archie and I were so ready to be done. Whoever wins, we just wanted a good night's sleep. I almost passed out on Jay Leno's couch [the next day]. It felt like such a grueling process, but I look back now and it was such a small moment in time. It's really hard to process. There's a unifying thing between you and the fans of this juggernaut of a TV show. It's worked out so far, but it's an amazing, funny thing.

What comes with being an American Idol?

DC: A 180-degree change. I still kind of get shocked when I talk to people about where I am in my life. My house—it struck me the other day, that I have a house. Before *Idol,* I was paying $200 a month to sleep on someone's couch. I think about all the people who did favors for me. Whether it was recording something or playing in my band for free or giving me a job. Now being able to pay it forward, that's the stuff that I really love. The best thing is just being in a position to have someone give me a chance to have a voice. I started playing in a band at fifteen and it was such a rare thing to have a known band bring an unknown onstage and give them a chance. To be in a position now where I'm on the other side of that and I can help out acts that are small and give them a chance, that's awesome.

DAVID COOK

- **HOMETOWN:** Blue Springs, Missouri
- **AUDITION SONG:** "Living on a Prayer" by Bon Jovi
- **WORDS TO LIVE BY:** *"It was like coming out of karaoke hell into a breath of fresh air, because it was original, daring, it stood out by a mile, and this is the sign of a great potential artist—someone who takes risks. Congratulations."* —Simon
- **LIFE AFTER** *IDOL***:** More than 50 million votes were cast for self-declared word nerd David Cook, and long after the victory cheers had subsided, he was still channeling the energy of finale night and twenty nearly flawless performances into a successful rock career. In fact, the week after his victory, David charted no less than eleven songs on the *Billboard* Hot 100 chart, breaking a record previously held by Bon Jovi.

Wasting no time in making a name for himself outside of the show, David teamed up with some of his own idols (like Our Lady Peace's Raine Maida and Collective Soul's Ed Roland) for his self-titled debut album, which was produced by Rob Cavallo (Green Day) and entered the *Billboard* album charts at number three in November 2008. It went on to sell 1.5 million copies and yield three singles as David hit the road for much of 2009 with The Declaration tour.

As David stayed true to his rock 'n' roll roots and his *Idol* family and fan base, his career continued its smooth and steady ascent as he scored much coveted bookings like *Saturday Night Live*, where he performed his hit song "Light On," and *Good Morning America*'s Summer Concert Series, where he performed the late-era Fleetwood Mac number "Little Lies" with season eight's Kris Allen and Adam Lambert. David even reteamed with his season seven runner-up, David Archuleta, for a concert together in Manila in the Philippines.

While he's clearly happy as a clam onstage, offstage David has weathered some trying times in recent years. His brother Adam, who had long suffered from brain cancer, succumbed to the disease in May 2009. David honored his

late brother during a return visit to *Idol* for the season eight finale, where he sang "Permanent" and made the live version available for download with all proceeds going to fund brain cancer research. He's undertaken similar fundraising initiatives with Race for Hope and the Shadow Buddies Foundation, and also traveled to Ethiopia in 2010 with Idol Gives Back partner the United Nations Foundation.

David's much-anticipated second album, on which he cowrote every song, was produced by Matt Serletic (Matchbox 20.)

DAVID ARCHULETA

- **HOMETOWN:** Murray, Utah
- **AUDITION SONG:** "Waiting on the World to Change" by John Mayer
- **WORDS TO LIVE BY:** *"I'm really proud of him and where he seems to be at as a person, and his singing is just beautiful."* —Mariah Carey
- **LIFE AFTER** *IDOL***:** If anyone's made a lasting impression on *Idol* both before and after appearing on the show, it would be young David Archuleta, who was first introduced

to the top ten back in season one, when he wowed the crew—and especially Kelly Clarkson—at a tour stop with his awe-inspiring a capella rendition of "And I Am Telling You I'm Not Going" from *Dreamgirls*. In addition to his winning the juniors version of *Star Search 2*, the experience would make the sixteen-year-old hopeful among the most seasoned of the class of 2008, skills that would come in handy when launching Archie's own post-*Idol* career.

Indeed, after signing with Jive Records in June 2008, David's debut album, released in November 2008, made a big splash, entering the *Billboard* 200 at number two, propelled by the success of its first single, "Crush," which sold 166,000 downloads its first week out. The album has since moved more than 750,000 copies. The following year, he released *Christmas from the Heart*, a collection of holiday classics.

David spent most of the spring of 2009 on tour performing his own headlining shows as well as opening for Demi Lovato. But not one to limit himself solely to music, David also devoted

time to honing his acting chops, following appearances on Disney's *Hannah Montana* and Nickelodeon's *iCarly*, and sharpening his writing and interviewing skills while working on a book, *Chords of Strength: A Memoir of Soul, Song, and the Power of Perseverance*, released in 2010.

David racked up the frequent-flyer miles that year as he crisscrossed the country attending songwriting sessions in Nashville, Los Angeles, and New York. The end result: Archie's much anticipated second album, *The Other Side of Down*, which shows the deeper side of Archie, as evidenced on tracks like "Things Are Gonna Get Better" and "Good Place." To that end, after the disastrous earthquake in Haiti, he jetted down to Miami to join Gloria Estefan and a host of Latin American artists for Somos El Mundo 25 Por Haiti, the Spanish version of We Are the World 25, whose proceeds benefited Haiti relief. And David still hopes to one day release an album in Spanish, his mother's native tongue, to which we say, *No tener que esperar*. Or, it couldn't come soon enough.

SYESHA MERCADO

* **HOMETOWN:** Sarasota, Florida

* **AUDITION SONG:** "Think" by Aretha Franklin

* **WORDS TO LIVE BY:** *"Stellar! Unbelievable! I'm loving it! Blazing hot!"* —Randy

* **LIFE AFTER *IDOL*:** Syesha Mercado strutted on the *Idol* stage as if she'd been singing on it her entire life, and while she spent more time in the bottom three than she would have liked, there was no doubt her future called for a spotlight in front and a full band behind her. Which is exactly what transpired a year after her third-place finish on *Idol*. Landing the role of Deena Jones in the touring production of *Dreamgirls*, Syesha hit the road in 2009, bringing her Broadway-ready moves and soulful sound to audiences all over America, including New York's famed Apollo Theater. Back home in Sarasota, she attended Florida International University in Miami, where she met her fiancé, classmate Hess Wesley.

JASON CASTRO

* **HOMETOWN:** Rockwall, Texas

* **AUDITION SONG:** "Once in a Lifetime" by Keith Urban

* **WORDS TO LIVE BY:** *"You have just got it. You're great with the camera. . . . It was effortless, you have charisma, I thought it was terrific."* —Simon

* **LIFE AFTER *IDOL*:** Following his fourth-place finish, some of Jason's season seven performances became among the most popular songs in the country. His cover of "Hallelujah," for example, catapulted the Jeff Buckley version onto the iTunes charts and did the same for Israel Kamakawiwo'ole's "Somewhere Over the Rainbow." Still, Jason Castro took some time figuring out what came next in his music career. And while he may have been a man of few words while doing interview segments for *Idol*, as an ambitious songwriter, he was anything but.

Jason's talents were immediately noticed by Atlantic Records, who signed him to a "360 deal," taking a vested interest in his recordings, touring, and merchandising. The label first released an EP, *The Love Uncompromised*, in January 2010, followed by his self-titled full-length three months later, featuring songs cowritten by the likes of John Fields (Jonas Brothers), Guy Chambers (Robbie Williams), and Kara DioGuardi. Jason returned to television in February 2010 to perform two tracks from the album on *The Bachelor* at wedding of Jason Mesnick and Molly Malany, but he would soon hit the road for a long string of dates in the U.S., the Philippines, and Malaysia.

Also that year, Jason married his longtime girlfriend, Mandy Mayhall. The two settled in Dallas, Texas, some twenty miles away from his hometown of Rockwall. Jason continues to perform all over the world, while also working on his follow-up album.

BROOKE WHITE

* **HOMETOWN:** Mesa, Arizona

* **AUDITION SONG:** "Like a Star" by Corinne Bailey Rae

* **WORDS TO LIVE BY:** *"Brooke was really good. I thought she had a sweet, warm way about her. . . . There's an honesty about Brooke that I really liked."* —Dolly Parton

* **LIFE AFTER *IDOL*:** Making it to the number-five spot on America's biggest singing competition brought Brooke White's unique singing style to a national audience, something she'd dreamed about since she was a kid first learning to play piano and guitar. And so after her finale duet with Graham Nash and the season seven summer tour, Brooke went back to doing what she loves: writing songs and performing live no matter how big or small the audience.

In 2009, Brooke signed with Sanctuary Management and went to work on her debut album, *High Hopes & Heartbreak*. Originally released as an iTunes exclusive, the album was partially backed by Randy Jackson, who partnered with Brooke to form June Baby Records. It wouldn't be the first creative business venture she'd delve into. A year later, Brooke announced the launch of *The Girls with Glasses* (www.thegirlswithglasses.com), an online talk show devoted to some of her favorite subjects, including fashion, music, and culture, though, as she first revealed during her *Idol* audition, she has yet to watch an R-rated movie.

CARLY SMITHSON

* **HOMETOWN:** San Diego, California

* **AUDITION SONG:** "I'm Every Woman" Chaka Khan

* **WORDS TO LIVE BY:** *"There's probably nowhere else that I feel more at home than on the stage. So as much as I'm missing everything at home, I'll give it up to be here on* American Idol *because this is really what I wanna do."*—Carly Smithson

* **LIFE AFTER *IDOL*:** Having weathered the ups and downs of the music business long before trying out for *American Idol*, Carly Smithson has been both lucky and unlucky in her bid for rock stardom. Sure, she may have scored and lost a major label deal while still a teenager, and when she first auditioned for *Idol* in season five, the Ireland native was disqualified due to complications with her visa, but coming back for season seven was the golden ticket

she'd long waited for, and after Carly's sixth-place showing, she was well positioned to make it as a singer.

A year after her *Idol* run had ended, Carly teamed up with Ben Moody, formerly of the band Evanescence, to form a new group called We Are the Fallen, which put Carly—and her instantly recognizable wail—front and center and allowed her the opportunity to shine not just as a vocalist but a songwriter. Their Universal Republic debut, *Tear the World Down* (which included two Carly originals), was released in May 2010 just as the band hit the road in support of hard rockers like HIM and Saving Abel.

KRISTY LEE COOK

* **HOMETOWN:** Selma, Oregon

* **AUDITION SONG:** "Amazing Grace" by Lee-Ann Rimes

* **WORDS TO LIVE BY:** *"Your voice is sounding much stronger. You're growing."* —Paula

* **LIFE AFTER *IDOL*:** She was season seven's budding country star who famously took a Beatles classic ("Eight Days a Week") and turned it into a banjo romp, but America didn't

hold it against Kristy Lee Cook. Sure, she was one of the bottom two that week and next, but in the end, fans kept her in the competition for another month before sending her home.

But Kristy wasted no time taking her career to the next level. She signed with Arista Nashville, where she'd once been a developing artist, and released her debut album, *Why Wait*, featuring the tongue-in-cheek single "15 Minutes of Shame" in September of 2008. But six months later, she parted ways with the label in order to pursue other avenues both in country music and the TV world. In fact, Kristy joins the handful of Idols who've managed to segue their time on-screen into a hosting stint. In 2010, the lifelong horse lover helmed the Outdoor Channel's countdown show, *10 Best*, as well as *Goin' Country* on the Versus network, which documents her love of hunting.

As for her music, Kristy landed a new deal with Broken Bow Records (home to Jason Aldean and James Wesley) in August 2010, with plans to release her second album in 2011.

MICHAEL JOHNS

* **HOMETOWN:** Buckhead, Georgia

* **AUDITION SONG:** "I've Been Loving You for Too Long" by Otis Redding

* **WORDS TO LIVE BY:** *"You sound as good as you look."* —Paula

* **LIFE AFTER *IDOL*:** The Australian-born rocker made an early exit from the top twelve but not without leaving his mark on season seven. Among Michael Johns's new fans: legendary arranger-producer-songwriter (and *Idol* mentor) David Foster, who invited him to appear on the star-studded *Hit Man: David Foster & Friends* special in December 2008, and songwriter Diane Warren, who gave Michael a key endorsement by writing a song that appeared on his debut album. That record, 2009's *Hold Back My Heart*, debuted at number twenty-two on the *Billboard* 200 and featured the soulful grit that he'd exhibited time and time again on the *Idol* stage. That year, Michael also contrib-

uted to the Shaun White documentary *Don't Look Down*. But even with all these successes (and the stumbles, like the two major label deals he landed and then lost before auditioning for *Idol*), there's a heavier—one might say grungier—side to Michael who's a lifelong Pearl Jam fan. Is it still clawing its way out? Rock fans on multiple continents hope to find out when he releases new music in 2011.

RAMIELE MALUBAY

* **HOMETOWN:** Miramar, Florida

* **AUDITION SONG:** "(You Make Me Feel Like) A Natural Woman" by Aretha Franklin

* **WORDS TO LIVE BY:** *"She's got a spunk, she's got the personality. The fact that she's little ain't gonna stop her from doing big things."* —Dolly Parton

* **LIFE AFTER *IDOL*:** She may have been little,

but there was no doubt Ramiele Mulabay had a big voice—so much so that it carried her to the top ten in one of the most talent-heavy lineups *Idol* had ever seen. But after making it to ninth place on season seven, Dolly Parton Week got the best of this aspiring R&B singer. Ramiele's post-show plans focused on her Philippines heritage as she made her way to Southeast Asia for a performance with the *Pinoy Idol* finalists. Back home in Florida, Ramiele sang the national anthem in Las Vegas preceding the Manny Pacquiao and Miguel Ángel Cotto fight at the MGM Grand and continues to keep fans abreast of new plans by vlogging on her official YouTube channel.

CHIKEZIE EZE

* **HOMETOWN:** Inglewood, California

* **AUDITION SONG:** "All the Woman I Need" by Luther Vandross

* **WORDS TO LIVE BY:** *"I was thoroughly entertained—who knew?!"* —Randy

* **LIFE AFTER *IDOL*:** The good-natured Nigerian-born Chikezie was on his second *Idol* attempt when he advanced to the top ten on season seven. His silky vocal styling and jokey demeanor made him a judge's favorite from the start, and kept audiences entertained for five weeks straight. After the show and summer tour,

Chikezie scored a couple of key TV bookings, appearing on the popular soap *General Hospital* in 2009 and hosting an *American Idols: Where Are They Now* special for TV Guide channel. The following year, he participated in Idol Gives Back by helping at a Los Angeles food bank located mere miles from where he grew up.

AMANDA OVERMYER

* **HOMETOWN:** Mulberry, Indiana

* **AUDITION SONGS:** "Turtle Blues" by Janis Joplin; "Travelin' Band" by Creedence Clearwater Revival

* **WORDS TO LIVE BY:** *"You really are an old Janis Joplin sixties revival thing and I love it!"* —Randy

* **LIFE AFTER *IDOL*:** With a born-to-be-wild stage stance, a fierce skunk-colored 'do, and a grit to her voice, Amanda Overmyer took *Idol* to eleven on season seven. Appropriately enough, that number was also her final position in the top twelve lineup, though it didn't slow her down one bit once she made her exit. Days after the season seven finale, Amanda debuted four original songs at the Whiskey a Go Go on L.A.'s famed Sunset Strip. A few months later, she played her biggest gig (not counting *Idol*): a hometown show for more than 10,000 people in Mulberry, Indiana. In 2009, Amanda released her debut, *Solidify*, a record that fit right into her hard-rock wheelhouse. The avid motorcycle enthusiast continues to perform all over the country, though it usually takes four wheels to get her from gig to gig.

DAVID HERNANDEZ

* **HOMETOWN:** Glendale, Arizona

* **AUDITION SONG:** "Ain't Too Proud to Beg" by The Temptations

* **WORDS TO LIVE BY:** *"When I sing, it comes from my soul. I've been through a lot in my life . . . so when I sing it's an escape for me."* —David Hernandez

* **LIFE AFTER *IDOL*:** He made it only as far as the top twelve, but David Hernandez continues to keep his *Idol* family close. Shortly after season seven wrapped, he joined fellow finalist Chikezie along with season two's Kimberley Locke and season three's Diana DeGarmo for a twenty-city *Idol* holiday trek. In 2009, he joined another package tour, this time featuring season six's Gina Glocksen, along with season eight's Michael Sarver and Alexis Grace, and self-released his first Christmas album, *This Christmas*. David has also seen his share of headlining slots, including a residency at an upscale Scottsdale, Arizona, nightclub, and major opening gigs, like when he warmed up for John Legend at the Declare Yourself Inaugural Ball in Washington, D.C., in January 2009, with A-listers like Jessica Alba and Jamie Foxx in attendance.

Greatest Hits

★ ★ ★ SEASON SEVEN ★ ★ ★

BILLIE JEAN

DAVID COOK

MARCH 25, 2008

It's long been a hotly contested topic among David Cook fans: Which of his twenty *Idol* performances is the absolute best? Lionel Richie's "Hello," the first to showcase his originality? David's moving version of Roberta Flack's "The First Time Ever I Saw Your Face," which was Simon's pick for the top three week? Collective Soul's "The World I Know," David's choice for the final two? Where most can agree is that his grungy rendition of Michael Jackson's "Billie Jean"—inspired by a Chris Cornell cover—is not only what put him on the *Idol* map, but likely secured his place in the finale. "You're probably the most bold contestant we've ever had," said Randy of David's "blazin' molten hot" performance. "You might be the one to win the whole lot!" Simon simply called it brave. "It could've either been insane or amazing," he said, "and it was amazing."

IMAGINE

DAVID ARCHULETA

FEBRUARY 26, 2008/MAY 20, 2008

As an end cap to the second week of the guys' semifinals performances—theme: the seventies—no one was expecting seventeen-year-old David Archuleta to deliver such a nuanced, mature take on John Lennon's idyllic "Imagine." It was a strong early showing that he'd encore for the finale, and one that prompted a teary Paula to predict, "You're destined for superstardom." Some three months later, she would tell young Archie, "You left me speechless as I was when I first heard you sing this song. You were stunning tonight."

ONE ROCK & ROLL TOO MANY

SYESHA MERCADO

MARCH 29, 2008

Andrew Lloyd Webber brought the drama to *Idol* as guest mentor on the top six week, which in turn kindled the Broadway spark inside Syesha Mercado, who delivered a knockout version of the *Starlight Express* staple. She began the party-time romp atop a grand piano and ended it sashaying with Rickey Minor and members of the *Idol* band! The performance yielded high praise from the judges, especially Simon who remarked, "That was, uh, very sexy," before declaring it one of Syesha's "strongest performances so far."

YOU'RE SO VAIN

BROOKE WHITE

FEBRUARY 27, 2008

If season seven had one no-brainer it would be Brooke White doing a song by Carly Simon, her musical doppelganger. As it turned out, audiences didn't have to wait long. Brooke opted for the classic kiss-off hit "You're So Vain" as her second proper performance—on the small stage for 1970s Week, aka the girls' top ten semifinals—and her first (nervously) playing acoustic guitar. While it wasn't aimed directly at the sole Brit on the panel (though he was sure It was), SImon told Brooke, "I absolutely loved it," noting that "it connected, you sang it very well, and this is the reason why we put you through to the latter stages." Brooke's response? A flabbergasted "Wow."

HALLELUJAH

JASON CASTRO

MARCH 5, 2008

Idol vIewers and judges alike had yet to decide whether the soft-spoken dreadlocked Jason Castro was worthy of season seven's top twelve when he chose to sing one of Simon Cowell's all-time favorite songs, the iconic "Hallelujah," during the last round of semifinals. But all doubt went out the window with Jason's delicate delivery, despite hitting a shaky, albeit emotional, ending. Simon called the rendition "absolutely brilliant," inspiring an encore performance by Jason on Finale Night, this time without the bum last note.

THE LETTER

CARLY SMITHSON AND MICHAEL JOHNS

MAY 21, 2008

She was a rocker who could wail like nobody's business; he was an Australian by way of Atlanta with serious soul and swagger, and together on Finale Night, they were duet partners who took chemistry and intensity to another level. Carly Smithson and Michael Johns traded verses on the hard-driving Box Tops hit "The Letter" against a bright red backdrop that only intensified the fierceness of their superhot performance. It was the last night of season seven, the final hour—little pressure (although it's still live TV), zero judgment, all fun, and a standout showing among a star-heavy lineup.

BREAKING
the INSTRUMENT
BARRIER

OUTSIDE OF TAYLOR HICKS'S HARMON-
ICA ACCOMPANIMENT TO HIS OWN SEA-
SON FIVE TOP TWENTY-FOUR WALK, IT
WASN'T UNTIL SEASON SEVEN THAT CON-
TESTANTS WERE OFFICIALLY ALLOWED
TO PLAY INSTRUMENTS DURING THEIR
IDOL PERFORMANCES. THE RESULT: A
WHOLE NEW MIXED BAG OF TALENT.

JASON CASTRO:

He was the first contestant to ever strum a six-
string on the American *Idol* stage, performing
The Lovin' Spoonful's "Daydream" during season
seven semifinals, and whether it was his trusty
acoustic guitar on Beatles Night, or the ukulele he
learned to play a week before his showstopping
rendition of "Over the Rainbow," Jason Castro
made an indelible mark on *Idol* for years to come.

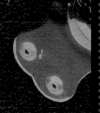

BROOKE WHITE:

Season seven's blonde-haired, blue-eyed beauty had a sound that could have come straight out of 1978, and the chops to back it up. Whether Brooke White was rocking the grand piano on the Police's "Every Breath You Take" or the acoustic guitar for Carly Simon's "You're So Vain," her performances were nothing short of moving.

DAVID COOK:

A white Les Paul guitar fit David Cook like a glove and allowed the season seven winner to deliver some of his most memorable performances, from the power chord–heavy version of Lionel Richie's "Hello" to his talk box take on The Beatles' "Day Tripper" and rousing version of The Who's classic "Baba O'Riley." Even more inspiring? The initials AC emblazoned on the head, in honor of his brother Adam, who was battling brain cancer.

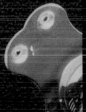

SCOTT MACINTYRE:

"The piano is part of who I am as an artist," said season eight's Scott MacIntyre, who counts award-winning singer-songwriter Billy Joel as one of his idols. So naturally, when it came time to show off his own skills, Scott often shared the stage with an old friend: the baby grand.

MATT GIRAUD:

Long before he auditioned for *Idol*, season eight's Matt Giraud paid the bills by tickling the ivories at various Kalamazoo, Michigan, watering holes and hotels. Once he got to Hollywood, Matt continued to jam nightly, wowing an audience of millions with his soulful singing style and undeniable skills.

KRIS ALLEN:

Like David Cook before him, season eight winner Kris Allen used his six-string to offer a unique twist on ubiquitous pop hits like Kanye West's "Heartless." The strategy paid off time and time again, prompting judge Kara DioGuardi to gush, "When you play your guitar, it's a whole other side of you."

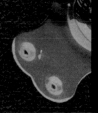

CASEY JAMES:

With the blues coursing through his veins, Season nine's resident guitar virtuoso was the incomparable—and adorable—Casey James, who could rock an infectious groove on an acoustic, electric, mandolin, and everything in between. Look no further than his country-fied twist on the cougar anthem "Mrs. Robinson" or John Lennon's pining "Jealous Guy" for proof of Casey's versatility.

CRYSTAL BOWERSOX:

Season nine's last girl standing was rarely without an acoustic guitar, but Crystal Bowersox could also handle the harmonica, as she showed time and time again on standout performances like her top twenty-four bow (Alanis Morissette's "One Hand in My Pocket") and final three rendition of "Come to My Window," originally sung by Crystal's own idol, Melissa Etheridge, whose signature happens to adorn the street-worn wood of her six-string.

LEE DEWYZE:

As a fan of classic folk acts like Simon and Garfunkel and Cat Stevens, season nine winner Lee DeWyze took his strumming seriously and was almost always seen with an acoustic guitar, both on the *Idol* stage and off. But perhaps most memorable of Lee's performances was the unexpected bagpipe accompaniment he chose for The Beatles' "Hey Jude."

American Idol

SEASON 7

BACKSTAGE PASS

1 /I

CHAPTER 14: **JUDGES AND MENTORS**

14

KARA DIOGUARDI 101

She came to *American Idol* with the reputation of a proven songwriter who had something to say, and after two years judging alongside Simon Cowell and Randy Jackson (with longtime friend Paula Abdul rounding out the panel in 2009, and comedienne Ellen DeGeneres in 2010), Kara DioGuardi got her point across.

So how did this respected music business insider find herself seated at America's most familiar table? It was all thanks to Kara's impressive industry cred, which included writing dozens of hits for the likes of Christina Aguilera, Pink, Kelly Clarkson, and Enrique Iglesias; owning a publishing company (Arthouse Entertainment); and holding a senior executive title at Warner Bros. Records. Because Kara had worked with many of the biggest names in music, she was a natural fit for the country's biggest singing competition.

Kara put her New York–bred moxie on full display during the audition rounds—taking on Bikini Girl in season eight and encouraging Casey James to ditch his shirt in season nine—and when it came time to go live, she was no less impactful with her words. There was the empathetic Kara, who would preface her critique with a gentle "sweetie," the realistic Kara, who would matter-of-factly tell a hopeful that singing wasn't his calling, and finally Kara the cheerleader, who would throw her weight behind the contestant with the most radio potential.

Her stay on the show was short-lived—just two seasons—but there's no doubt Kara made her mark on *Idol* by bringing seriousness to the competition. After all, millions of dollars are invested in the winner's career and debut album, which very well may include the purchase of a Kara DioGuardi track or two.

KARA DIOGUARDI:

SHE WRITES THE SONGS THAT IDOLS SING

If there's been one consistent *Idol* credo from over the years, it's to keep things in the family. No wonder hit-songwriter-turned-judge Kara DioGuardi wrote almost thirty songs for various *Idol* alumni, like . . .

KELLY CLARKSON:

BREAKAWAY: "Walk Away," "Gone," "Where Is Your Heart," "You Found Me," "I Hate Myself for Losing You," "Hear Me" • ALL I EVER WANTED: "I Do Not Hook Up"

CLAY AIKEN:

MEASURE OF A MAN: "The Way"

DIANA DeGARMO:

BLUE SKIES: "Dream, Dream, Dream," "The Difference In Me," "Till You Want Me," and "Blue Skies"

CARRIE UNDERWOOD:

PLAY ON: "Undo It" and "Mama's Song"

BO BICE:

THE REAL THING: "It's My Life," "Remember Me," and "The Real Thing"

TAYLOR HICKS:

TAYLOR HICKS: "Heaven Knows" and "Give Me Tonight"

KATHARINE McPHEE:

KATHARINE MCPHEE: "Open Toes," "Love Story," "Not Ur Girl," "Each Other," "Neglected," and "Home" • UNBROKEN: "Had It All" and "Terrified"

KRIS ALLEN:

KRIS ALLEN: "No Boundaries"

DANNY GOKEY:

MY BEST DAYS ARE AHEAD OF ME: "I Still Believe"

ALLISON IRAHETA:

JUST LIKE YOU: "No One Else"

DAVID ARCHULETA:

DAVID ARCHULETA: "To Be with You"

ELLEN DEGENERES 101

In the thirty-plus years that Ellen has been making audiences laugh, she's accomplished a lot: countless sold-out comedy clubs; award-winning roles on television; stints hosting the Emmys, Grammys, and Oscars; not to mention *The Ellen DeGeneres Show*, which has made Ellen the most successful daytime talk show host since her pal Oprah Winfrey came on the scene. In 2010, she added *American Idol* judge to her impressive résumé when she replaced Paula Abdul and joined Simon Cowell, Randy Jackson, and Kara DioGuardi for the show's ninth season. Hired to bring a different perspective to the group, the avid *Idol* fan made no secret of her love of music, and her tumultuous and awe-inspiring career path has made her an expert of sorts in the art of winning over the public.

Dubbed "the Female Seinfeld" when her ABC sitcom was at the top of the ratings heap, by the turn of the millennium, Ellen, who had come out as a lesbian in 1997, had ascended to one of *Forbes'* "5 Most Influential Women in Media." She uses that influence as a spokesperson for CoverGirl and American Express, as well as her many charitable endeavors. The Louisiana native has worked tirelessly to campaign for funds on behalf Hurricane Katrina victims. To date, her show has raised more than $10 million for Katrina efforts and more than $50 million for other causes, like animal rights, global warming, and breast cancer. Her "heart of gold" was fully displayed during her one season as an *Idol* judge, where she wore the "nice judge" label with honor while also managing to throw in plenty of her trademark Ellen zingers ("As a matter of fact, yes, I have loved a woman") and it seems that DeGeneres's dip into the musical pond won't be her last: She recently announced the launch of her own record label, Eleveneleven, and signed her first artist, twelve-year-old YouTube sensation Greyson Chance.

"If I had that much confidence when I was eleven . . . "

"Most people would say don't take on such a big song, but they also said don't mix sleeves with a blanket and look at the Snuggie, it's huge!"

"There was a brief time in the seventies that I believed I could fly."

"I love bananas. Sometimes a banana is not quite ripe and you're like, 'Oh I wish it was riper, because I'd like to eat that banana right now . . . ,' You just need to ripen."

Ellen DeGeneres's stint as a judge on *Idol*, while brief, yielded an arsenal of season nine jokes and zingers that are sure to endure—certainly in the minds of these contestants.

"I like that you're holding onto the mullet and you're not gonna let it go."

"The wardrobe changes—it's like a Cher concert in here!"

"You made the word 'fire' two syllables, which I thought was gr-eat."

"That was a very horny song—there's a lot of horns in it!"

"I was expecting a tiny bit more from you. It almost didn't come together, like a hospital gown."

"You're like the soup of the day: sometimes I like the soup and sometimes I don't like the soup. And I've liked your soup, I have! But today I didn't like your soup. I'm sorry."

"I still am such a huge fan that I am thinking about getting your name tattooed on my neck."

"As a mutter of fact, yes, I have loved a woman."

NEIL PATRICK HARRIS, SEASON 9: The *How I Met Your Mother* star is an accomplished song-and-dance man himself (look no further than his surprise musical number on the 2010 Academy Awards or his Broadway appearances in *Cabaret* and *Assassins*), so judging talent was a natural fit; he joined the judges during the Dallas auditions.

JOE JONAS, SEASON 9: Taking his judging duties seriously in the Dallas auditions, heartthrob Joe Jonas delivered just the right amount of sound advice coupled with encouragement to future finalist contestants Tim Urban and Paige Miles.

SHANIA TWAIN, SEASON 9: Country star Shania Twain was all over *Idol* during season nine, showing up as a guest judge at the Chicago auditions, where eventual winner Lee DeWyze and runner-up Crystal Bowersox sang in front of the panel for the first time, then later in the season as the group's mentor and theme inspiration.

KRISTIN CHENOWETH, SEASON 9: A Broadway background along with her bubbly personality instantly endeared Kristin Chenoweth to *Idol* hopefuls at the Orlando auditions. Among them: top twelve finalists Lacey Brown and Aaron Kelly.

VICTORIA BECKHAM, SEASON 9: Posh Spice herself sat in on the season nine auditions in Denver and Boston, looking ravishing as ever as she doled out pop star advice to droves of *Idol* hopefuls. The British Beckham proved to be gentler than fellow countryman Simon Cowell, giving out plenty of compliments.

AVRIL LAVIGNE, SEASON 9: The outspoken punk-pop princess showed off her musical expertise when she filled the guest judge spot for season nine's Los Angeles auditions.

JAMIE FOXX, SEASON 8 *AND* SEASON 9: Appearing as an *Idol* mentor for the second time during season nine, the multitalented Oscar-winning actor, singer, and superstar was the perfect coach for Songs of the Cinema night.

LADY GAGA, SEASON 9: For her second *Idol* appearance, Lady Gaga brought a slew of sexy male dancers to accompany her on the hit song "Alejandro."

IDOL GUEST STARS

Many of the leading hit makers in the music industry and Hollywood have appeared on the *Idol* stage and behind the judges table. Here are some who gave their advice throughout the past ten years.

DIANE WARREN

MARK McGRATH

GENE SIMMONS

KENNY LOGGINS

LL COOL J

BRANDY

DIANA ROSS

PETER NOONE & LULU

GWEN STEFANI

TONY BENNETT

JENNIFER LOPEZ

MARTINA MCBRIDE

JON BON JOVI & DAVID BRYAN

BARRY GIBB

MARIAH CAREY

ANDREW LLOYD WEBBER

NEIL DIAMOND

RANDY TRAVIS

SMOKEY ROBINSON

QUENTIN TARANTINO

JAMIE FOXX

SLASH

VICTORIA BECKHAM

MARY J. BLIGE

KRISTIN CHENOWETH

AVRIL LAVIGNE

KATY PERRY

NEIL PATRICK HARRIS

JOE JONAS

MILEY CYRUS

ADAM LAMBERT

ALICIA KEYS

SHANIA TWAIN

15

SEASON EIGHT'S TOP TWO showdown pitting the showman against the singer-songwriter involved two completely opposite entities: In one corner you had Adam Lambert, a flamboyant fashion- and image-conscious performer with years of musical theater to his name. In the other you had the laid-back, unassuming Kris Allen, acoustic guitar almost always in hand, and most comfortable wearing a plaid flannel shirt. The unlikely combination made for one of the most entertaining, not to mention unpredictable, finales in *Idol* history.

Of course, it wouldn't be America's favorite singing competition without an element of surprise, and year eight boasted several. The first: a fourth judge, hit songwriter Kara DioGuardi, who had worked with the likes of Kelly Clarkson, Enrique Iglesias, and Celine Dion, would lend her expert ear to the panel. Another was the introduction of the judges' save, which was allowed only once and had to be used prior to the top five. And for the first time ever, the show featured a top thirteen rather than a top twelve (this in addition to a top thirty-six instead of the customary twenty-four).

All that talent made for uber-confident finalists such as Allison Iraheta, a soon-to-be seventeen-year-old with fierce vocal chops, and Matt Giraud, a part-time dueling piano player who was as stage ready as they come, while stunners Alexis Grace and Megan Joy were relatively new to the world of pro performers but screamed star potential.

Hardships were faced, too, not the least of which centered on final three contender Danny Gokey, who had tragically lost his wife, Sophie, a year earlier to complications from heart surgery. And there was Scott MacIntyre, the legally blind contestant who'd spent years toiling away at the piano trying to make it as an independent artist. Ditto for Michael Sarver, an oil rig worker trying to take care of his family. In fact, the financial meltdown of the previous year weighed heavily on season eight, which called off plans of "Idol Gives Back" out of concern that struggling Americans could not donate as generously.

But where *Idol* did give plenty was in providing pure entertainment—from Kris Allen's acoustic twist on Kanye West to Adam Lambert's dramatic reworking of Johnny Cash, it was a season of reinvention and one that would ultimately bid adieu to the show's biggest cheerleader, Paula Abdul.

CLASS of
09

SEASON 8 YEARBOOK

"i 'm genuinely beginning to think you've got a shot in this competition." —Simon Cowell

KRIS ALLEN

"Shoe Salesman"

SEASON 8
WINNER!
2009

ANOOP DESAI

"Student"

MATT GIRAUD

"Dueling Piano Player"

DANNY GOKEY

"Church Music Director"

ALEXIS GRACE

"Musician-Mom"

ALLISON IRAHETA

"Student"

MEGAN JOY

"Font Designer"

"It's like you've been singing for four hundred years. That is from God. You can't teach that. —Kara DioGuardi

'With every performance, it's like watching the Olympics and you're our Michael Phelphs."
—Paula Abdul

SEASON 8
RUNNER-UP
2009

ADAM LAMBERT
"Stage Actor"

SCOTT MACINTYRE
"Student"

JASMINE MURRAY
"Student"

JORGE NÚÑEZ
"Student"

LIL ROUNDS
"Customer Service Rep"

MICHAEL SARVER
"Oil Rig Roughneck"

WINNER'S CIRCLE

Looking back with the season eight champ

What was your first encounter with the judges like?

Kris Allen: I actually saw Simon and Randy in the bathroom before I auditioned. I was waiting and had to pee really bad, so they told me I could go to the bathroom and I don't think I was supposed to be in that bathroom because Randy and Simon both walked in!

Were there competitors that stood out from the very beginning?

KA: We all knew Adam would do well. We knew Danny would do well. We thought Lil Rounds would go far. She has a huge voice. Those were the people I thought were in it to win it.

Your acoustic guitar version of Kanye West's "Heartless" was considered a turning point in the competition. Were you worried about how the performance would be received?

KA: It was a risk. I always play guitar and used to put hip-hop songs to it; people would sing along and love it. "Heartless" is a song I liked and it was popular at the time. I had been listening to it and was, like, "Hey, I can do that." I knew people would either love it or hate it.

Is there an instant bond between *Idol* winners past and present?

KA: Kind of. It's definitely not like Kelly Clarkson called my cell phone as soon as I won. But you see each other and it's this understanding that you went through the same thing and people think of you in a certain way when you win *Idol*.

From a guy's perspective, what was the glam squad experience like?

KA: I was probably a stylist's worst nightmare, because I don't care. Especially at that point, I really didn't care—I wanted to wear jeans and T-shirts. The great thing is the stylists were so nice. They always wanted you to be comfortable and to have input in what your look will be. I was open to it. I was like, "Hey, these jeans are tighter than usual, but OK . . . " I had to get used to that stuff, but overall it was a great experience.

KRIS ALLEN

- **HOMETOWN:** Conway, Arkansas

- **AUDITION SONG:** "A Song for You" by Leon Russell

- **WORDS TO LIVE BY:** *"If you can't feel a Kris Allen performance and he doesn't move you, there's something wrong with you. You have a way of creating an intimate bond with everybody in the audience, you make us feel like you're singing it to us and that's so hard to do."* —Kara DioGuardi

- **LIFE AFTER *IDOL*:** Following his season eight win, Kris Allen's version of the Kanye West tune "Heartless," along with his coronation song "No Boundaries," reached the top twenty on *Billboard*'s Hot 100 chart. In November 2009, he released his self-titled debut album, which spawned the radio staple "Live Like We're Dying," then hit the road, opening for the likes of Keith Urban, Maroon 5, and OneRepublic. Offstage, Kris continued to pursue another of his passions: charity. In February 2010, he traveled to earthquake-ravaged Haiti to lend his name and a helping hand. Upon his return, Kris headed back to the *Idol* stage for an emotional rendition of The Beatles' "Let It Be," donating all the proceeds from iTunes sales of his season nine performance to the relief effort.

ADAM LAMBERT

- **HOMETOWN:** San Diego, California

- **AUDITION SONG:** "Bohemian Rhapsody" by Queen

- **WORDS TO LIVE BY:** *"Never in the history of American Idol, all seven seasons leading up to now, have we ever seen someone so comfortable and seasoned on that stage. I don't even notice the stage, because I'm transfixed on you! Your innate ability to know who you are as an artist and marry fashion with music—you do that. You've got the whole package going on. And I believe with all my heart we'll be seeing you run all the way to the end."* — Paula

✳ **LIFE AFTER *IDOL*:** Adam Lambert spelled out his future in the title to his debut album, *For Your Entertainment* (released November 2009), and, as usual he did not disappoint. Within months of his second-place finish, Adam raised eyebrows—and the nation's collective blood pressure—with a risqué performance of the title track at the 2009 American Music Awards. A smash single, "Whataya Want from Me," and more major appearances followed, including multiple stints on *The Tonight Show*, and in no time Adam had graduated from the TV stage to major venues across the United States and Europe, making him one of the most successful *Idol* alums—and the first to be asked back to the show as a mentor.

DANNY GOKEY

✳ **HOMETOWN:** Milwaukee, Wisconsin

✳ **AUDITION SONG:** "I Heard It Through the Grapevine" by Marvin Gaye

✳ **WORDS TO LIVE BY:** *"The true mark of an artist is when you can hear somebody even with your eyes closed and know exactly who they are, and you possess that gift among so many others."* —Paula

✳ **LIFE AFTER *IDOL*:** With the summer 2009 American Idols Live! Tour winding down came news that Danny Gokey was joining the Sony Nashville roster, alongside fellow *Idol* alums Carrie Underwood and Kellie Pickler. His debut album, *My Best Days,* released in March 2010, landed at number four on the *Billboard* charts—the highest debut by a country music newcomer in nearly two decades. Soon after, Danny was opening for country's reigning star duo, Sugarland. A widower who's always kept his late wife close to his heart, Danny has continued to devote time to Sophia's Heart, a foundation set up in her name, that helps disadvantaged children.

ALLISON IRAHETA

✳ **HOMETOWN:** Glendale, California

✳ **AUDITION SONG:** "(You Make Me Feel Like)

A Natural Woman" by Aretha Franklin

✳ **WORDS TO LIVE BY:** *"My life right now could not get any better. It's a dream and I hope I don't wake up."* —Allison Iraheta

✳ **LIFE AFTER *IDOL*:** Season eight's last girl standing wasn't about to go out with a whimper. Signed to Jive Records soon after her fourth-place elimination, Allison Iraheta released her bombastic debut, *Just Like You,* in December 2009 to positive reviews. Three singles, "Friday I'll Be Over U," "Scars," and "Don't Waste the Pretty," followed, along with a host of promotional and live appearances (several with fellow alums Kris Allen and Adam Lambert, which gave rise to the nickname Kradison) taking her as far east as Indonesia. Waiting for Allison upon her return: an opening slot on Adam's *Glamnation* tour!

MATT GIRAUD

❋ **HOMETOWN:** Kalamazoo, Michigan

❋ **AUDITION SONG:** "I Don't Wanna Be" by Gavin DeGraw

❋ **WORDS TO LIVE BY:** *"You are talented, sexy, amazing, authentic, I'm blown away."* —Paula

❋ **LIFE AFTER *IDOL*:** After Matt Giraud got the judges' save and extended his *Idol* stay by two weeks, he took his soul man act on the road for the summer tour, incorporating classic R&B numbers like Otis Redding's "Hard to Handle" and Ray Charles's "Georgia on My Mind" into his set. Upon his return, Matt continued to pound the piano pavement, performing sold-out shows in his home state and eventually making his way back to the *Idol* stage for a piano duel with follow top ten contestant Scott MacIntyre. He recorded a song with jazz singer Anna Wilson in 2010, which shot to number one on the iTunes jazz charts, and has been hard at work in Nashville on his own album.

LIL ROUNDS

❋ **HOMETOWN:** Memphis, Tennessee

❋ **AUDITION SONG:** "All I Do" by Stevie Wonder

❋ **WORDS TO LIVE BY:** *"You've got unbelievable vocals and you definitely know who you are."* —Randy

❋ **LIFE AFTER *IDOL*:** As a mother of three, Lil Rounds certainly had her hands full, but that didn't slow down the multitasking R&B diva one bit. In between studio sessions for her debut album, Lil became a spokesperson for Amp Pro hair products and gave acting a try, hoping to appear on the stage and screen in the future.

ANOOP DESAI

❋ **HOMETOWN:** Chapel Hill, North Carolina

❋ **AUDITION SONG:** "Thank You" by Boyz II Men

❋ **WORDS TO LIVE BY:** *"You have tender, honest, amazing, sweet vocals. You touch my heart."* —Paula

❋ **LIFE AFTER *IDOL*:** Anoop Desai returned to

a hero's welcome in his home state of North Carolina and hit the ground running, receiving a key to the city of Chapel Hill, performing locally, and even making a cameo on Food Network's *Food: Impossible* when the show visited his alma mater, UNC. Anoop released his debut album, *All Is Fair* (featuring the single "My Name," which was cowritten by season six top twelve finalist Brandon Rogers), in May 2010.

SCOTT MACINTYRE

* **HOMETOWN:** Scottsdale, Arizona

* **AUDITION SONG:** "And So It Goes" by Billy Joel

* **WORDS TO LIVE BY:** *"Whatever challenges you've faced to get here, I'm so proud and happy that you did. You're a genius at the piano. You blessed us all with your gift and you're one of our finest."* —Paula

* **LIFE AFTER *IDOL*:** Scott MacIntyre picked up right where he left off after his eighth-place elimination—at the piano. The visually impaired talent recorded his debut album, *Heartstrings*, which he released in March 2010. That same month, he and fellow finalist Matt Giraud returned to the *Idol* stage to reprise a crowd favorite from the summer tour, Billy Joel's "Tell Her About It."

MEGAN JOY

* **HOMETOWN:** Sandy, Utah

* **AUDITION SONG:** "Can't Help Lovin' Dat Man" from *Show Boat*

* **WORDS TO LIVE BY:** *"I don't wanna change who I am. That's what I wanna do, even if it's not safe. I'm gonna walk the plank and it's my plank, so let's party."* —Megan Joy

* **LIFE AFTER *IDOL*:** Blonde, bold, and beautiful, with a distinctive singing style that wowed the judges, Megan Joy found her voice on the competition and put it to work soon after, recording nearly twenty-five songs for her yet-to-be-released debut album. Equally unique was her look, which drew the attention of modeling agencies, but Megan's first priority has remained the same since well before her *Idol* days: raising her son, Ryder.

MICHAEL SARVER

* **HOMETOWN:** Jasper, Texas

* **AUDITION SONG:** "Thank You" by Boyz II Men

* **WORDS TO LIVE BY:** *"So you are the complete opposite of Ryan Seacrest, aren't you?"* —Simon

* **LIFE AFTER *IDOL*:** Michael Sarver went from working the fifth most dangerous job in the world to defying odds of an entirely different sort and making it to *Idol*'s top ten. Dream fulfilled? Hardly. The prolific songwriter and father of two has embarked on a country career, signing with Dream Records and releasing his debut single, "Ferris Wheel," in April 2010.

ALEXIS GRACE

* **HOMETOWN:** Memphis, Tennessee

* **AUDITION SONG:** "Dr. Feelgood" by Aretha Franklin

* **WORDS TO LIVE BY:** *"You are a naughty girl and I liked it."* —Kara DioGuardi

* **LIFE AFTER *IDOL*:** After Simon Cowell compared her to Kelly Clarkson, Alexis Grace's early exit went down as one of the most surprising

eliminations in *Idol* history, but it didn't stop the young mom from pursuing her dreams. Upon returning home, Alexis landed a regular gig appearing on Memphis radio station Q107.5 while also working on a country album and touring with *Idol* alums like tenth-place finalist Michael Sarver.

JORGE NÚÑEZ

* **HOMETOWN:** Carolina, Puerto Rico

* **AUDITION SONG:** "My Way" (in Spanish) by Frank Sinatra

* **WORDS TO LIVE BY:** *"You were born to sing. You have that gift of touching people when you sing, because you really believe it. It comes from your heart."* —Kara DioGuardi

* **LIFE AFTER *IDOL*:** Unconfirmed

JASMINE MURRAY

* **HOMETOWN:** Columbus, Mississippi

* **AUDITION SONG:** "Big Girls Don't Cry" by Fergie

* **WORDS TO LIVE BY:** *"Music is the biggest part of my life. I want to be onstage, I want to have that feeling."* —Jasmine Murray

* **LIFE AFTER *IDOL*:** As season eight's youngest competitor (just sixteen at the time of her audition), Jasmine Murray first had to finish high school before continuing on her musical path. The beauty pageant veteran has been performing locally while figuring out her next post-*Idol* move.

Greatest Hits

⊛ HEARTLESS

KRIS ALLEN

MAY 12, 2009

Kris always delivered onstage, but his acoustic version of West's techno-heavy hit, "Heartless" floored the judges and possibly sealed his fate as *Idol*'s next champion. Simon said, "It has all changed after that performance." Kara called his performance "bold, brave, and fearless," and Randy noted "I liked that version better than The Fray's or Kanye's."

⊛ MAD WORLD

ADAM LAMBERT

APRIL 7, 2009

Adam's moody rendition of Tears For Fears' "Mad World" was so mesmerizing, he performed it twice! First during Songs from the Year You Were Born Week, which garnered a standing ovation from Simon himself, and again during his top two bout for the *American Idol* title. The encore performance on finale eve earned him an "A+" from Randy, which Simon reaffirmed by noting, "I always thought this was your best performance of the competition." Kara called him an "extraordinary singer" and "an incredible artist." Paula agreed, simply stating, "I think you did a brilliant job."

⊛ PART-TIME LOVER

MATT GIRAUD

APRIL 7, 2009

When Matt Giraud delivered his smooth and slowed-down version of the Stevie Wonder classic, he out-sang the other seven contestants by a mile. Simon called Matt's vocals "the best of the night" and Paula had only two words: "Standing-O." Audiences agreed and Kara called it "incredible on every level."

CRY BABY

MAY 6, 2009

The fiery red-haired rocker defended her place in the final four with this mind-blowing rendition of Janis Joplin's classic "Cry Baby." Simon complimented Allison's "complete confidence and terrific vocals." Randy gushed, "You can sing your face off! You can sing anything!" And Paula added, that "if they ever do a Janis Joplin biopic, you've got the role." Too bad it was the performance that would ultimately send Allison home, while her elimination night encore would cause countless viewers to second guess their decision.

YOU ARE SO BEAUTIFUL TO ME

MAY 12, 2009

Danny Gokey's Contestant's Choice pick of Joe Cocker's classic love song made a strong impression on the judges during top three night. But while Simon called it "a vocal master class" and Kara described his rendition as "stunning" and "amazing," it wasn't enough to carry Danny into the final two. Still, Randy's words echoed on: "You showed you could really, really, really sing."

WALKIN' AFTER MIDNIGHT

MARCH 17, 2009

The tattooed beauty dug her heels in during Grand Ole Opry Week to deliver her finest effort. Mentored by country legend Randy Travis, Megan delivered a nearly flawless performance of Patsy Kline's "Walkin' After Midnight" shortly after being hospitalized for the flu, prompting Simon to joke, "You should have the flu every week." Despite her illness, Megan looked smashing in a flowing dress that perfectly draped her frame, and sounded even better, with Randy calling her performance "impressive."

DIRTY DIANA

MARCH 10, 2009

As top twelve debuts go—or in season eight's case, top thirteen—Alexis Grace's fierce version of this lesser-known Michael Jackson hit gave her instant frontrunner status. Making the brooding number even darker was her sexy, all black get-up, but in the end, momentum from this performance would only see her through to the next round, and one week shy of the top ten.

American Idol

SEASON 8

BACKSTAGE PASS

16

SEASON NINE SAW PLENTY OF CHANGES at the judges' table. Gone was Paula Abdul, who had bowed out a few months earlier. In her place was talk-show host Ellen DeGeneres, armed with a pocketful of jokes and ready to face the music for a one-season stint. To her left was veteran songwriter Kara DioGuardi in her second and last year on the show. And a little farther down, Simon Cowell, who announced early in the season that he would be leaving at the end of *Idol*'s ninth run. It all made for a feeling of finality on one side of the room while on the stage twelve wide-eyed hopefuls embarked on a road traveled by few but leading to good things.

To put it in perspective, after the dizzying array of showmanship that was season eight, the following year's crop of contestants faced the daunting reality of constant comparisons. Eternally quirky Siobhan Magnus bared the brunt of it, thanks to her octave-defying wail, which immediately harkened back memories of many an Adam Lambert showstopper. As for winner Lee DeWyze and runner-up Crystal Bowersox, their brand of acoustic-minded rock was more reminiscent of Kris Allen's *Idol* run, complete with plaid flannel shirts.

What stood out in the season nine crew, however, was the undeniable musical skills that every hopeful in the top twelve displayed, be it Michael Lynche, whose deep R&B leanings and urban savvy screamed "star power" from the minute he took the *Idol* stage, or Andrew Garcia, whose folky twist on pop hits made him a household name and instant YouTube star. Casey James, too—he was a guitarist who could hold his own at any blues bar in his home state of Texas. Ditto for Didi Benami, who bravely took on a challenging Fleetwood Mac classic while simultaneously strumming on live TV.

In fact, if any top ten could go down in *Idol* history as the year of the six-string, it would be the season nine bunch, which, thanks to their song choices, made for a mostly mellow vibe to the competition (again, not counting Siobhan, who made a spectacle out of every number she tackled, from head to toe). Look no further than Aaron Kelly, who never met a ballad he didn't like. Or Tim Urban, who took a page straight out of the *Idol* handbook when he chose the moving "Hallelujah" for his top twenty-four performance, accompanied solely by his acoustic guitar.

But even in its ninth season, *Idol* still had its share of new experiences. For one thing, it was the first time a former contestant—season eight runner-up Adam Lambert—returned to the show as a mentor, and it was a year that featured an insane array of megastar guest performances, from Lady Gaga to Usher, Justin Bieber, Rihanna, and beyond. Though the stars of this show were and always will be the contestants, there was no doubt *Idol* had arrived.

CLASS *of* 10

SEASON 9 YEARBOOK

"MamaSox, you know why they call you that? Because you just schooled all those contestants.
—Kara DioGuardi

SEASON 9
RUNNER-UP
2010

DIDI BENAMI

"Waitress"

CRYSTAL BOWERSOX

"Musician-Mom"

LACEY BROWN

"Church Event Director"

SEASON 9
WINNER!
2010

LEE DEWYZE

"Paint Sales Clerk"

ANDREW GARCIA

"Musician-Dad"

CASEY JAMES

"Construction Worker"

"Chicks dig a guy who can actually play the guitar and sing." —Usher

AARON KELLY

"High School Student"

MICHAEL LYNCHE

"Personal Trainer"

SIOBHAN MAGNUS

"Glassblowing Apprentice"

PAIGE MILES

"High School Student"

KATIE STEVENS

"High School Student"

TIM URBAN

"Singer"

WINNER'S CIRCLE

Looking back with the season 9 champ

Of the past winners, who do you relate to most?

Lee DeWyze: Kris Allen and David Cook. Kris is a down-to-earth, cool guy. I can definitely have a BBQ with him. Musically, I'd say David. People always compare us because I play the guitar, but he is a completely different artist than me. I respect the hell out of both those guys and I know what they've been through in this process.

What was your most memorable performance of the season?

LD: "The Boxer" was cool. It was one of the first songs I learned how to play on guitar, which is why that song means so much to me. After I learned it and for a long time, it was one of the only songs I knew. And even now, I'll pop that on my iPod and it puts me in a really good place.

What do you think Ellen DeGeneres brought as a judge to season 9?

LD: I think she brought a little sensitivity to the show and comic relief. All the judges were great, and I appreciate what they do, but at the end of the day it's the fans who decide everything.

Do you feel like the competition has changed you?

LD: Everybody that's come through has started in one place and ended up in another. Do I think I've changed? No, but has my opinion on a lot of things changed? Yes. People grow, discover new things about themselves and the world. *Idol* has opened my eyes and made me realize that a lot of the little things I was getting upset about and used to bother me are just so small. I was sitting in my store mixing paint, the same way Casey was at home doing construction, and Crystal was being a mom do. None of us thought we would be on national TV in a year. So it has kind of changed me, but not who I am deep down.

Tell us about your early interactions with the judges.

LD: Simon ripped me apart during Hollywood Week. He said some stuff where I was, like, "Damn, this guy's mean!" But I took everything into consideration, and as time's gone by, I've realized he's just someone who's been around and seen a lot of things in the music industry. He noticed me and that's what I care about.

LEE DEWYZE

✳ **HOMETOWN:** Mt. Prospect, Illinois

✳ **AUDITION SONG:** "Ain't No Sunshine" by Bill Withers

✳ **WORDS TO LIVE BY:** *"You have so much soul and depth to you which we're seeing more and more of. We're seeing better and better from you which is surprising because I already think you're great."* —Ellen

✳ **LIFE AFTER *IDOL*:** When it came to working on his first album, *Live It Up*, the season nine champ wasted no time getting going in the studio. Helping define that husky sound were in-demand songwriter-producers John Shanks, Toby Gad, and David Hodges, who put an airy flare to Lee's pop-rock flavor, starting with the single "Sweet Serendipity," which he premiered on *On Air With Ryan Seacrest*. It was a collaborative effort in the end, and Lee was able to claim an *Idol* first: he co-wrote every song on the record.

Elsewhere in his post-*Idol* career, Lee nabbed a Teen Choice Award for "Choice Male Reality TV Star" in August 2010. A month later, he played a homecoming concert in Arlington Heights, Illinois, attended by over 20,000 fans.

CRYSTAL BOWERSOX

✳ **HOMETOWN:** Elliston, Ohio

✳ **AUDITION SONG:** "Piece of My Heart" by Janis Joplin and Big Brother and the Holding Company

✳ **WORDS TO LIVE BY:** *"I think that mainstream music right now needs a little pick-me-up, just get back to the real roots of music."* —Crystal Bowersox

✳ **LIFE AFTER *IDOL*:** The soulful singer revered for her raw, natural talent came up just short of an *Idol* win, but she's been going full speed ever since. After releasing her show-stopping cover of Patti Griffin's "Up To The Mountain" on iTunes, Crystal gathered her repertoire of original songs, assembled an all-star band (including guys who had played with Billy Joel) and went to work on *Farmer's Daughter*,

her debut album. Its first single, "Hold On," was written by Kara DioGuardi and Nickelback's Chad Kroeger. In between studio sessions, she campaigned on behalf of juvenile diabetes research—even appearing at the White House—and spoke out against bullying on Anderson Cooper. Now well on her way to a successful career in music and having achieved her ultimate goal—to provide a good life for her son, Tony—Crystal lived out another of her dreams when she married longtime friend and fellow musician Brian Walker in October 2010.

CASEY JAMES

* **HOMETOWN:** Fort Worth, Texas

* **AUDITION SONG:** "Slow Dancing in a Burning Room" by John Mayer

* **WORDS TO LIVE BY:** *"He had a swagger. He had a confidence that said 'I belong here.' He's a guy I'd definitely keep an eye on, winner or not."* —Usher

* **LIFE AFTER *IDOL*:** With guitar in hand, Casey James continues to melt hearts and blow minds long after his third place finish on season nine. Staying true to his country-blues roots, Casey signed with Sony Music Nashville at the end of the *Idol* summer tour, then packed his dogs and guitars and moved to Music City where he began working on his debut album. For a guy who'd never watched *Idol* before auditioning, the show sure took him a long way.

MICHAEL LYNCHE

* **HOMETOWN:** Astoria, New York

* **AUDITION SONG:** "Unchained Melody" by the Righteous Brothers

* **WORDS TO LIVE BY:** *"Here's a big, big guy with muscles and that's what we see, but inside that muscular guy is a little tiny sensitive—I call him Tiny Mike to myself, he's so sensitive and so sweet."* —Ellen

* **LIFE AFTER *IDOL*:** Following his fourth place finish, Michael re-joined his wife and beautiful baby girl Layla Rose at home in Queens, New York, then waved goodbye—again—to his family as he embarked on the *Idol* summer tour. Big Mike's three-song set included show favorites like "This Woman's Work" and Brian Adams'

"Have You Ever Really Loved a Woman," his top four week duet with Casey. Even after returning from the trek, Mike's *Idol* affiliation continued when he started working on new music, with help from Ruben Studdard.

AARON KELLY

* **HOMETOWN:** Sonestown, Pennsylvania

* **AUDITION SONG:** "The Climb" by Miley Cyrus

* **WORDS TO LIVE BY:** *"Your mom was absolutely right—you were definitely born to sing."* —Randy

* **LIFE AFTER *IDOL*:** With vocals beyond his years, fresh-faced Aaron made it to fifth place and got to perform on the finale with the Bee Gees. After making the TV show rounds and touring with his fellow season niners, Aaron moved to Nashville to embark on a country career in earnest.

SIOBHAN MAGNUS

* **HOMETOWN:** Barnstable, Massachusetts

* **AUDITION SONG:** "Love of My Life" by Queen

* **WORDS TO LIVE BY:** *"I'm a big fan of people who march to the beat of their own drum and you certainly do and I support that because I think you really should always honor who you are, because you are special, you are really talented and really special. Always remember that."* —Ellen

* **LIFE AFTER IDOL:** She may have gone home earlier than expected, but Siobhan Magnus has had plenty to smile about since her sixth place elimination. Immediately following the finale, where she sang alongside Alice Cooper and the Bee Gees, Siobhan got to meet her own personal idols, Hanson, at the official season nine wrap party. She later said of the experience, "It was better than I could have ever dreamed of."

While her early elimination was a shock to many fans, Siobhan got redemption from an unexpected ally: David Letterman. After her *Late Show* performance of "Paint It Black,"

he proclaimed, "As far as I'm concerned, you should be the American Idol."

On the American Idols LIVE! Tour, Siobhan's set, which included songs like No Doubt's "Spiderwebs" and Muse's "Stockholm Syndrome," was a huge crowd pleaser every night. Equally comfortable performing to a packed arena as she is atop a float at her hometown parade, Siobhan remains one of the show's most memorable contestants.

TIM URBAN

* **HOMETOWN:** Duncanville, Texas

* **AUDITION SONG:** "Bulletproof Weeks" by Matt Nathanson

* **WORDS TO LIVE BY:** *"It's like a mouse picking a fight with an elephant. You're not gonna win, but it doesn't matter because you're gonna smile, the audience is gonna vote for you, nobody cares, and you'll be here next week so, well done!"* —Simon

* **LIFE AFTER IDOL:** After several close calls, "Teflon Tim" Urban took his last *Idol* bow with

the Goo Goo Dolls' "Better Days," but there were plenty ahead for him as well. After returning home from playing packed houses on the *Idol* tour, Tim was given a hero's welcome in his native Ducanville, Texas. In fact, the town mayor declared September 3, 2010, Tim Urban Day, while also presenting him with a key to the city. Wasting no time getting his own music out to the world, in November of that year, the well-coiffed Tim began releasing a song a day on iTunes, all singles from his debut EP, *Heart Of Me*. He went on to release six singles that week, including "Blur," "Lullaby," and "Wheels Touch Down."

Angeles to focus on her music career. Currently, the unsigned artist is working with heavy-hitter songwriters like David Hodges.

ANDREW GARCIA

* **HOMETOWN:** Moreno Valley, California

* **AUDITION SONG:** "Sunday Morning" by Maroon 5

* **WORDS TO LIVE BY:** *"I appreciate everything and I'm glad I'm here. I'm glad I've been through what I've been through."* —Andrew Garcia

* **LIFE AFTER *IDOL*:** Like his buzzed about show entrance, Andrew's nights on the Idol tour offered more "Straight Up" fun—both on stage and off. Today, his performance of the

KATIE STEVENS

* **HOMETOWN:** Middlebury, Connecticut

* **AUDITION SONG:** "At Last" by Etta James

* **WORDS TO LIVE BY:** *"You have a natural gift. I mean, you have ridiculous chops."* —Kara

* **LIFE AFTER *IDOL*:** She was sent packing along with Andrew Garcia in the season's only double elimination, and after making the rounds on the talk show circuit, the dough-eyed teen joined her friends on the American Idols LIVE! Tour where she performed "Here We Go Again" by Demi Lovato and "Fighter" by Christina Aguilera. Once the forty-four-city trek wrapped in August, Stevens made the bold move to Los

Paula Abdul classic is still one of the most watched Youtube clips of Idol's ninth season, and the number one request Andrew gets, no matter where he goes. In fact, you could say Andrew's built a second career on the web's biggest video portal, where he's constantly posting new clips. Andrew currently lives in Pasadena with his wife and son.

DIDI BENAMI

* **HOMETOWN:** Knoxville, Tennessee

* **AUDITION SONG:** "Hey Jude" by The Beatles

* **WORDS TO LIVE BY:** *"Everybody's seen this really sweet emotional side to me but I've been in L.A. for a really long time and I don't think I would've lasted this long if I didn't have this thing that keeps me alive in this town."* —DIdi Benami

LIFE AFTER *IDOL*: Didi had a reputation for tearing up, when she's actually a really happy-go-lucky person. OK, so it didn't always come through on television, but her fierce fashion sense and stellar voice certainly did. Picking up where *Idol* left off, she sang Kara DioGuardi's, "Terrified" on TV and throughout the *Idol* summer tour, after which Didi returned to Los Angeles to pursue a career in music (collaborating with singer-songwriter Jason Reeves, among others) and acting. She plans to release an album in 2011.

PAIGE MILES

* **HOMETOWN:** Naples, Florida

* **AUDITION SONG:** Unaired

* **WORDS TO LIVE BY:** *"I think you have such great star quality and such great presence on stage."* —Ellen

* **LIFE AFTER *IDOL*:** This die-hard Michael Jackson fan was among the first in the top twelve to be sent home after her performance of Phil Collins' "Against All Odds" failed to wow voters. Paige did, however, return to the *Idol* stage twice, once for Idol Gives Back and again during the season nine finale.

LACEY BROWN

* **HOMETOWN:** Amarillo, Texas

* **AUDITION SONG:** "Somewhere Over the Rainbow" by Judy Garland

* **WORDS TO LIVE BY:** *"Where you're very good is you that know where the cameras are, how to look—it feels like you've been doing this a long time."* —Simon

* **LIFE AFTER *IDOL*:** She just made the cut-off for the top twelve, only to be sent home in week one after her rendition of The Rolling Stones' "Ruby Tuesday" fell flat. Still, the Texan beauty continues on her musical path, performing all over the country, and wants to give acting a try as well.

⊛ STRAIGHT UP

ANDREW GARCIA

HOLLYWOOD WEEK, 2010

Andrew Garcia pulled the Paula card on day one of Hollywood Week when he performed her 1988 breakthrough hit, "Straight Up," to the judges' delight. Putting an unlikely twist on the pop number, Andrew had only an acoustic guitar as an accompaniment. "That was genius," judge Kara DioGuardi exclaimed as the other top twenty-four hopefuls cheered along. "Paula would be screaming and yelling and clapping and dancing and diving!" Though he got compared to season eight's Adam Lambert for "taking a song and flipping it," Andrew didn't quite have the same staying power and finished in eighth place.

⊛ THIS WOMAN'S WORK

MICHAEL LYNCHE

MARCH 10, 2010

His daughter, Laila Rose, was born during Hollywood Week, and days later Michael Lynche indulged his sensitive side with a gorgeous rendition of the 1989 Kate Bush classic (which was a hit for Maxwell in 2001) that made Kara break down in tears. "I've never cried after hearing something like that," she said. "It's so relevant for you right now I can feel it." The audience felt it, too, as Big Mike was swiftly ushered into the top twelve the following night.

⊛ RIHANNON

DIDI BENAMI

MARCH 10, 2010

Ellen DeGeneres's reaction to the top twelve contender's interpretation of Fleetwood Mac went something like this: "Yes, indeedy, Didi!" In fact, the lullabylike performance, which featured Didi plucking along on acoustic guitar, was praised by three of season nine's four judges, including Simon, who took issue with Randy's assertion that she didn't have a "moment." "The 'wow moment' was actually the whole performance," Simon insisted. "It was really well balanced and I thought it was a brilliant choice of song . . . well done."

LET IT BE

KATIE STEVENS

APRIL 6, 2010

By the time the top nine came around, seventeen-year-old Katie Stevens had been in the bottom three twice, but she was spared the red lights following her moving Lennon-McCartney Week performance of "Let It Be," which Randy called her best ever. "Those were hot vocals . . . and that's why you're in the top nine," he said. Katie chose the inspirational song because "everybody can relate to it," she explained during her video package. Afterward, Katie breathed a sigh of relief along with a sense of accomplishment. "I wanted to come out here with a bang," she told the *Idol* camera. "And to hear the judges say that I deserve to be here and I'm blossoming is great."

PAINT IT BLACK

SIOBHAN MAGNUS

MARCH 16, 2010

Siobhan Magnus's top twelve entrance was as dramatic as they come. Seated on the *Idol* stairs, wearing a black cocktail dress and combat boots, she started the Rolling Stones' staple with a moody string-led melody and climaxed with her octave-defying rock star–ready wail and the deafening cheer of the crowd. The judges were clapping, too, with Kara recalling "flashbacks of Adam Lambert" and Simon declaring it "the standout performance of the night." No wonder Siobhan encored the song during the summer tour.

I CAN'T HELP FALLING IN LOVE WITH YOU

TIM URBAN

APRIL 13, 2010

Under the tutelage of mentor Adam Lambert, perpetual underdog Tim Urban received a much-needed boost during Elvis Presley Week when he took on the King's classic love song. Tim's sweet, unaffected delivery (even while Ryan Seacrest inexplicably waltzed with an audience member nearby) steered away from gimmicks and a flashy ending and cued one of Simon's more famous season nine lines: "You have managed to go from zero to hero."

CASEY JAMES

★ JEALOUS GUY

APRIL 6, 2010

Having already proven that he was adept at blues, country, and radio-friendly pop, Casey James finally wowed the judges with his twangy, stripped-down version of a John Lennon solo number. Its simplicity—an acoustic guitar melody complemented by a cello—brought out the song's inherent beauty and prompted Simon to call Casey's performance "the best of the night."

★ ME AND BOBBY McGEE

MARCH 23, 2010 / MAY 25, 2010

CRYSTAL BOWERSOX

The song Janis Joplin made famous was a natural fit for the rootsy Crystal Bowersox, who made it her calling card and performed it twice during the competition. In fact, Crystal was so comfortable with the tune, that she requested a homey carpet be rolled out for her top eleven turn (and got Ryan Seacrest to take a seat on it while reading her voting number). Simon compared her soulful delivery to Pink's, while Randy remarked, "This is what it's about!"

★ THE BOXER

APRIL 20, 2010 / MAY 25, 2010

LEE DEWYZE

One of the songs that catapulted Lee DeWyze to his *American Idol* win was this Simon and Garfunkel classic, which happened to be a longtime favorite of the former paint salesman's and served as an appropriate metaphor for his own musical crusade. Lee's first turn at "The Boxer" was during Inspirational Songs Week, when he took mentor Alicia Keys's advice to heart. "People have to feel like you are that boxer, you are that fighter," she said. The end result was so well received that Lee opted for a repeat performance on Finale Night.

American Idol

SEASON 9

BACKSTAGE PASS

CONTESTANTS
TALK BACK

Season nine's Siobhan Magnus mastered the art of the retort by continually insisting she wasn't just one thing that fit neatly into a little box. Of course, she's not the first top twelver to talk back and certainly won't be the last. Here, some more unforgettable contestant snap moments.

JUSTIN GUARINI, SEASON 1: He holds the distinction of being the first *Idol* contender to poll the crowd in response to a judge's jab. The performance in question? Justin's rendition of "Sunny" for 1960s Week. *"I really respect your opinion,"* said Justin turning to the audience, *"but what did you guys think?"* After getting heat for being disrespectful and perhaps a tiny bit pompous, Justin apologized the following week, telling the panel, "I got caught up in the moment. That's not me, that's not who I am and I wanna apologize to everyone."

KIMBERLEY LOCKE, SEASON 2: With a hiss to the finger, the sassy Kimberley Locke put Simon in his place early in the semifinals round. Criticizing her supposed lack of stage charisma, Simon said he'd give her 4.5 out of 10 for personality. Kim shot back, telling the judge he'd score "a well-deserved zero" and explaining how "when most people criticize other people, it means they're not happy with themselves." After the exchange, Simon awarded Kimberley an extra point, to which she responded, *"Wow, I would say thank you, but I just can't find it anywhere back there . . . I thought you were sexy; you suck."* Pow!

JOSH GRACIN, SEASON 2: Simon's lackluster reaction to Josh Gracin's Diane Warren Week performance of 'NSync's "That's When I'll Stop Loving You" wasn't what he was hoping to hear, but rather than let it tear him up, the poker-faced marine cracked, *"I'm respectful of elders."*

CONSTANTINE MAROULIS, SEASON 4: An early-in-the-season performance of The Black Crowes' "Hard to Handle" made Constantine Maroulis an instant favorite of female viewers coast to coast, but Simon wasn't impressed. "I could go to any bar across America and see a band with somebody of the same caliber as you and it wouldn't excite me," he said. Constantine's response was simple: *"I'll prove you wrong."*

MANDISA, SEASON 5: Simon mocked Mandisa's weight following her Chicago audition, but between that fateful day and Hollywood Week, she had plenty of time to reflect on the dis and in the end, found her peace with it. *"You hurt me and I cried,"* she told Simon just before making the top twenty-four. *"But I want you to know that I've forgiven you."* His response was uncharacteristically empathetic. "Mandisa, I'm humbled," said Simon. "Give me a kiss."

KEVIN COVAIS, SEASON 5: Some contestants have come to expect the worst of Simon, leaving no surprises. The crabby Brit criticized Kevin "Chicken Little" Covais's Stevie Wonder Week rendition of "Part-Time Lover." Kevin's response? *"It's alright,"* he said with a shrug. *"I wasn't expecting much from you anyway."*

CHIKEZIE, SEASON 7: Still horrified by the bright red suit Chikezie wore the week before, Simon just had to bring it up again, even after a moving rendition of Ray Charles's "I Believe To My Soul." "I liked my suit," Chickezie defended as Simon egged him on. *"Would I wear it again? I wore it on TV, can't wear it twice. Can't do a replay, only you'd do that!"* Nine "I'm sorrys" later, Chikezie only dug himself a bigger hole. "Just when I'm beginning to like you again, you become obnoxious."

DAVID COOK, SEASON 7: David Cook had yet to dazzle the judges in his second week of semifinals. The theme: music of the 1970s. His choice: Free's "All Right Now." Simon's reaction? "You don't have a lot of charisma, which is fine." Cook's retort: *"Fortunately, I don't have to win you over with my charisma, I have to win these people over."* This time, rather than grin and bear it, Simon snapped back. "I think I know by now the rules of the competition," Simon sneered.

CARLY SMITHSON, SEASON 7: Mariah Carey week was a challenge for all in the season seven top seven, but one contestant, rocker Carly Smithson, thought Simon was being especially harsh. *"I think you've been a bit hard on me,"* she said matter-of-factly. Simon explained: "Because I think you're potentially great and I just wanna give you that extra push sometimes." Sadly, that push came the following week, when Carly was shown the door.

NICK MITCHELL, SEASON 8: As the sassier version of himself, Nick Mitchell's alter ego Norman Gentle hurled his share of insults Simon's way, including this top twenty performance after which he called the British judge *"Sassy Pants."* And, of course, who could forget the Brit's unexpected mention of getting kicked and liking it, to which Nick snapped back, *"you mean the way you like it when Seacrest does it?"*

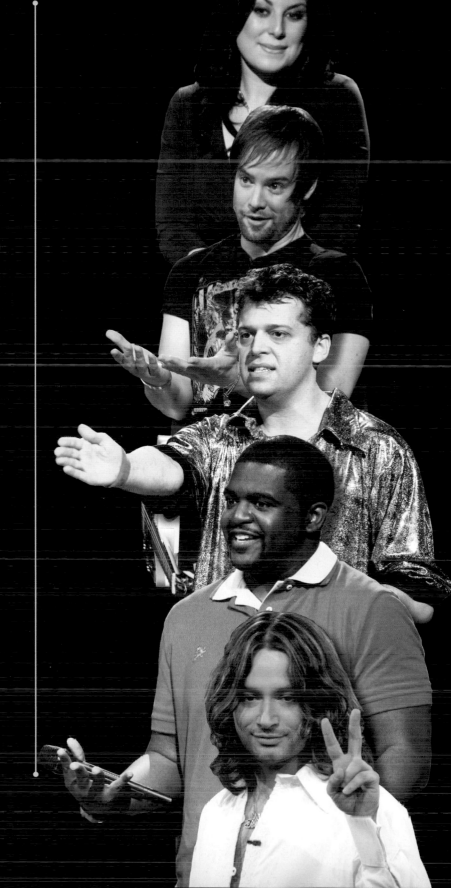

CELEBRATING A DECADE ON THE AIR

is a momentous occasion for any show, but rather than resting on its laurels, *American Idol* saw its tenth season as an opportunity for reinvention. Just like in previous years, the show was the talk of the nation months before any contestant took position in front of the judges, only this time there were new faces who brought their own styles and experiences to the biggest talent search of the decade.

The show had already proven it could find and launch bona fide stars, so it was no surprise that *Idol* would enlist two of the most successful artists in pop and rock history for its new judges panel: Jennifer Lopez, a triple threat who had already conquered the music world and added actress, trendsetter, entrepreneur, and all-around diva (in the best way) to her already impressive resume; and Aerosmith frontman, Steven Tyler, a rock legend whose songs have been performed on the *Idol* stage many times and have been entertaining audiences for years with his octave-defying vocals and undeniable rock star swagger. On the opposite end of the table was Randy Jackson, the seasoned *Idol* veteran who had seen and heard it all, yet still approached

every *Idol* hopeful with fresh ears and an open mind. And, of course, super-host Ryan Seacrest was back for another round of dream-making, his delivery sharper and snappier than ever.

Still, though some things had changed—including an update to the already spectacular stage, an extended Hollywood Week, the return of the judges' wild card round, and a shorter road from semifinalist to finalist—plenty of Idolisms stayed the same: Contestants still squealed at the sight of a golden ticket, Ryan continued to provide a sympathetic shoulder to cry on, and the ensemble cast and devoted crew members never stopped doling out time-tested advice on how to make it in the music world.

As for the contestants? What aspiring artist wouldn't jump at the chance to have an audience with international superstar Jennifer Lopez? Or to get singing tips from Steven Tyler, a man whose rock range knows no boundaries? You would have to be crazy, and sure, season ten's auditions brought out plenty of those, but many more truly talented performers with promise, sass, and determination—familiar qualities to all of *Idol*'s key players—also made their presence known. The result: simply inspiring.

PHOTOGRAPHY CREDITS

The Publisher wishes to thank:
FremantleMedia
19 Entertainment
American Idol Productions
FOX

ACKNOWLEDGMENTS

Shirley Halperin would like to thank Rebecca Kaplan, David Cashion, Sofia Gutierrez, and all the incredibly hard-working editors at Abrams Books. Much gratitude to Cortney Wills, my tireless intern on this project, and Michele Angermiller, who interviewed Taylor Hicks and helped write several pages. Roger Widynowski and Gina Orr, your support over the years is very much appreciated. Randy Jackson and Harriet Sternberg: love. Thanks to Paul Kepple and Ralph Geroni at Headcase Design for their top-notch art direction, James Ngo and the fine folks at FremantleMedia, Michelle Young, Michelle DeLeon and the staff at 19, and the *Idol* PR team, including Manfred Westphal, Eric Greene, Michael Cilnis, Chloe Ellers, Leslie Fradkin, and especially Jill Hudson. To *Idol* alums Blake Lewis, Constantine Maroulis, Jon Peter Lewis, Elliott Yamin, Bo Bice, Didi Benami, and Siobhan Magnus, I'm grateful for your friendship. To David Cook and Adam Lambert, bless you for shaking up the show in all the right ways. Seven publications have allowed me to cover the series as it raised the country's collective blood pressure on a weekly basis, among them *Us Weekly*, *Entertainment Weekly*, and the *Hollywood Reporter*. Those editors were key in recognizing what would become a pop culture phenomenon, so props for the foresight, Lori Majewski and Janice Min. And lastly, to Simon Fuller and the *Idol* creators and crew, thanks for bringing music into the living rooms of millions.

ABOUT THE AUTHOR

Shirley Halperin is a longtime music journalist who has covered *American Idol* since season one for no fewer than seven outlets, including *Us Weekly*, *Rolling Stone*, *Entertainment Weekly*, *Billboard*, *Teen People*, and the *Los Angeles Times*. She's currently the music editor at the *Hollywood Reporter*, where she continues to write about the show via the magazine's *Idol* Worship blog. Shirley is married to music producer Thom Monahan and based in Los Angeles.

Editor: Rebecca Kaplan

Designer: Headcase Design • www.headcasedesign.com

Art Director: Michelle Ishay

Production Manager: Jacquie Poirier

Library of Congress Cataloging-in-Publication Data:

Halperin, Shirley.

American Idol : celebrating 10 years / by Shirley Halperin.

p. cm.

Includes bibliographical references and index.

ISBN 978-0-8109-9830-8 (alk. paper)

1. American idol (Television program) I. Title.

ML76.A54H35 2010

791.45'72—dc22

2010048584

Abrams books are available at special discounts when purchased in quantity for premiums and
promotions as well as fundraising or educational use. Special editions can also be created to specification.
For details, contact specialmarkets@abramsbooks.com or the address below.

THE ART OF BOOKS SINCE 1949

115 West 18th Street
New York, NY 10011
www.abramsbooks.com